Y0-CAZ-024

Landscaping with
Bulbs

LANDSCAPING WITH BULBS

Series Concept: Robert J. Dolezal
Encyclopedia Concept: Barbara K. Dolezal
Managing Editor: Victoria Cebalo Irwin
Bulbs Factual Consultant: John E. Bryan
Photography Editor: John M. Rickard
Designer: Jerry Simon
Layout Artist: Barbara K. Dolezal
Photoshop Artist: Gerald A. Bates
Horticulturist: Peggy Henry
Photo Stylist: Peggy Henry
Proofreader: Ken DellaPenta
Index: Alta Indexing Service, El Cerrito, CA

Copyright © 2002
Creative Publishing international, Inc. and Dolezal & Associates
5900 Green Oak Drive
Minnetonka, MN 55343
1–800–328–3895
All rights reserved
Printed in U.S.A. by Quebecor World
10 9 8 7 6 5 4 3 2 1

President/CEO: Michael Eleftheriou
Vice President/Editorial: Linda Ball
Vice President/Retail Sales & Marketing: Kevin Haas

Home Improvement/*Gardening*
Executive Editor: Bryan Trandem
Editorial Director: Jerri Farris
Creative Director: Tim Himsel

Created by: Dolezal & Associates,
in partnership with Creative Publishing international, Inc.,
in cooperation with Black & Decker.
BLACK&DECKER. is a trademark of the Black & Decker
Corporation and is used under license.

Library of Congress Cataloging-in-Publication Data

Dolezal, Robert J.
  Landscaping with bulbs / author, Robert J. Dolezal ; photographer,
John M. Rickard.
    p. cm. -- (Black & Decker outdoor home)
  ISBN 1-58923-004-3 (pbk.)
  1. Bulbs. 2. Landscape gardening.   I. Title. II. Series.
  SB425 .D66 2002
  635.9'4--dc21
                                        2001047297

ISBN 1–58923–004–3

PHOTOGRAPHY & ILLUSTRATION

PRINCIPAL PHOTOGRAPHY:

JOHN M. RICKARD: All photographs except where otherwise noted below.

OTHER PHOTOGRAPHY AND ILLUSTRATION:

CORBIS: ©Michael Boys, 119 (mid); ©Nigel J. Dennis, 106 (top); ©Hal Horwitz, 98 (top), 111 (top), 123 (mid); ©Staffan Widstrand, 122 (top).

ROBERT DOLEZAL: pgs. 16 (bot), 17, 78 (bot L).

PHILIPPE FAUCON: pg. 112 (bot).

DAVID GOLDBERG: pg. 126 (top).

DONNA KRISCHAN: pgs. 2 (bot), 7 (top R), 14, 24, 26 (bot L), 28 (top), 29 (mid), 84, 100 (top), 101 (mid), 107 (mid), 111 (mid), 112, 120, 124 (top & mid), 125 (top), 128 (top).

NETHERLAND FLOWER BULB INFORMATION CENTER: pg. 97 (mid).

JERRY PAVIA: pgs. 96 (bot), 98 (mid & bot), 100 (bot), 101 (top), 107 (bot), 110 (top), 113 (mid), 115 (top & mid), 117 (bot), 123 (bot), 125 (mid), 126 (mid), 129 (top & mid), 130 (bot).

PHOTODISC IMAGE STOCK: pg. 75 (top R).

RUTH ZAVITZ: ©Ruth Zavitz, 110 (bot)

ILLUSTRATIONS: HILDEBRAND DESIGN

ACKNOWLEDGEMENTS

The editors acknowledge with grateful appreciation the contribution to this book of Brian Davis of Mt. Shasta Florist, Mt. Shasta, CA; Betsy Niles, Sonoma, CA; and the Netherlands Flower Bulb Information Center.

Landscaping with

Bulbs

Author
Robert J. Dolezal

Photographer
John M. Rickard

Series Concept
Robert J. Dolezal

Complete guide
to growing
beautiful bulbs

CREATIVE
PUBLISHING
international

MINNETONKA, MINNESOTA

www.creativepub.com

CONTENTS

INTRODUCTION

*W*hen springtime breezes first waft through groves of budding aspen, and tulips and crocus begin their rise out of newly warmed soil, gardeners everywhere should be reminded of the endless bounty that nature provides to those with the forethought to dream and act.

Spring bulbs are one such miracle. Late in autumn, as first frosts begin to brown the grass and leaves turn every shade and hue, we gardeners dream of spring's warmth and a new season for sharing beauty with our neighbors.

Out of net bags come the yield of our carefully saved bulbs, still dormant from their summer's rest. Raking aside the fallen leaves, we prepare the soil for planting, stopping for a moment to lean on our spade and admire the waning beauty of autumn crocus and cyclamen.

Working the soil until it is loose, we apply fertilizer, mix it in, and cover it with a blanket of fresh soil to separate it from our precious bulbs. Diagrams in hand, we begin to create our magic in patterns hidden beneath the soil.

> ❝ *When I go into the garden with a spade, and dig a bed, I feel such exhilaration and health that I discover that I have been defrauding myself all this time in letting others do for me what I should have done with my own hands.* ❞
>
> RALPH WALDO EMERSON

Our thoughts may drift at such moments to scenes of yesteryear, of hands held by a mother gently guiding a child's first daffodil into its planting bed. We may look past the rich soil to the times and places that we find only in our imagination, to friendships and experiences that are hidden in our secret heart.

Or we may, instead, be first-time gardeners trying out our hobby for size. We have long admired others' yards and now hope to create similar beauty in our own special spot.

Whether we choose from the many spring bulbs—longtime favorites for early, cheerful color—or the summer and autumn bloomers known for their sophistication and dignity, bulbs reward us with grace and beauty rarely found in other flowering plants.

Whatever our motivation, gardening with bulbs is an act of faith and a commitment to renewal. By bedding our hyacinth, squill, and lily-of-the-valley before winter's snows fall, by planting tulip, narcissus, and snowdrop into planters and pots, we reaffirm our trust that the cold days now upon us surely will wane and spring will come again.

The joy bulbs give is as much a reminder of our own rebirth as is a rainbow the fleeting memento of a storm's passage.

Planting bulbs is a testament to patience and reward gained through honest effort.

So, gardener, rest your hands on that shovel a bit longer, and take some time to reflect as you shoulder your task. By trusting the land and placing your love in your plantings, you are committing yourself to caring.

Your payback will be measured in more than a bulb garden filled with glorious blooms or the praise received from those who view it.

O

Make your garden and home a colorful showplace filled with blooming bulbs during every season of the year

Beautiful Bulb Landscapes

f all the garden flowers, bulbs are perhaps the most magical. They lie in wait, dormant beneath the soil for much of the year, only a promise of the glory that is to come. Then they seemingly explode in a blast of color that shakes us out of our winter doldrums.

Whether spring-, summer-, or autumn-blooming, bulbs are suitable for every garden. You can grow bulbs of every variety in their multitude as container plants, landscape flowers, and in natural gardens, while tender, tropical, and evergreen species are mainstays for houseplants. Besides true bulbs, plants that have corms, rhizomes, tubers, and tuberous roots are grouped loosely together under the broad classification of "bulbs."

Bulbs are found in nearly every locale of the populated world. They have a fascinating history, boast societies and clubs devoted to them, and have spawned industries that cultivate and supply a centuries-old worldwide demand for their flowers. They also have been the subject of many stories and even intrigue.

Two thousand years or more before the birth of Christ, anemone, iris, and lily appeared on palace frescoes painted by ancient Minoans at Crete and in the tomb paintings of the Egyptians. Bulbs traveled with the crusaders in the 1500s from the kingdom of Suleiman the Magnificent in Asia Minor to Austria, and then to Holland. It was there that collecting rare tulips reached its zenith during the early 1600s, with a single prized bulb fetching many years' salary, before climaxing in a manic market crash that demolished entire trade dynasties.

Since then, bulbs have been collected in the wild by explorers bound for Afghanistan, India, Persia, South Africa, Turkey, and Asia. They have been transported from tropical lands and icebound mountains alike. Trappers and traders swapped furs in North America for bulbs of trillium, Mariposa lily, and wood sorrel. Remember these interesting facts as you look at your spring blooms.

The passion for bulbs is one you'll share as you discover, choose, plant, and enjoy plantings—both inside your home and outdoors in your landscape—that you'll select from common, unusual, and rare bulb species.

The warmth you feel on a springtime day is a perfect complement to the deep yellow of 'King Alfred' daffodils and the welcome that you can expect at an entry door.

INDOOR AND FORCED BULBS

Both forced bulbs— those grown to bloom at a specific time— and other indoor bulb plantings enhance your home's decor during winter and early spring. Hyacinth (right), lily-of-the-valley (far right), and florist's amaryllis (below) are among the choices for indoor bulb plantings.

While bulbs are used widely in the landscape, in massed plantings, and as accents, they also can be enjoyed indoors [see Indoor Bulbs and Forcing, pg. 85]. Their welcome color and exquisite fragrance are a vivid antidote to winter's gray skies and snow-bearing winds.

You have many types of bulbs from which to choose for indoor displays, each with its own attributes. Most popular are spring bloomers that flower in the short days of winter. Many cold-hardy bulbs can be forced—coaxed into bloom at times other than their usual habit would permit—creating bouquets of living plants and cut flowers to bolster your spirit. Most spring bulbs are suitable for forcing: crocus, daffodil, freesia, grape hyacinth, hyacinth, narcissus, and tulip. More rarely seen spring bulbs round out this group, including bluebell, lily-of-the-valley, snowdrop, snowflake, starflower, trillium, and the lovely, shamrocklike wood sorrel.

Many summer- and autumn-blooming bulbs also are used as houseplants. They are widely planted because some of their species bloom in repeated waves, interwoven with periods of relative dormancy. Some examples are autumn crocus, cyclamen, miniature dahlia, gloxinia, summer hyacinth, lily, dwarf lily-of-the-Nile, Mexican tuberose, and windflower.

Tropical bulbs and evergreen species are good choices for year-round indoor enjoyment. They include colorful foliage plants as well as those loved for their flowers. Amaryllis, tuberous begonia, caladium, florists' cyclamen, perennial ginger, Amazon lily, orchid pansy, and squill are just a few examples. Provide warmth, ample sunlight, and, for some species, moisture and humidity similar to that found in their native regions.

Every room of your home will be more welcoming with bulbs providing a floral display. Bulbs are ideal for household use because many adapt well to container living. By planting a series of pots over a span of several weeks in autumn, you can have flowers in bloom all winter long. Plan for a storage space to keep the bulbs before and after they bloom. Consider how the scale of your bulb planting relates to your room, table, or shelf. A cozy corner near a window, while ideal for flat containers filled with diminutive crocus, would cramp a pot containing a dozen large tulips.

As you begin to plan for indoor bulbs, select varieties that are compatible with the color scheme of the rooms where you will place them. Bulbs tend to bright colors, though they include many examples that are either white or one of several muted pastels. Choose locations that will receive full sun while the bulbs are on display.

Citry apartment dwellers and others with limited space can garden outdoors by filling balconies, courtyards, patios, and exterior foyers with bulbs in containers. Decks are welcoming in spring when they are adorned with groups of pots filled

OUTDOOR CONTAINER BULBS

with crocus, hyacinth, paperwhite narcissus, and tulip. Entryways show off summer hardy and tuberous begonia, dahlia, lily, and dwarf lily-of-the-Nile, and window boxes filled with autumn crocus and cyclamen belie the coming winter with their cheerful blooms. Bulbs are the right choice for virtually every season, in homes of every size.

Outdoor container gardens are really plots grown in pots. Various bulbs require different planting conditions, and your choice of containers should accommodate their needs. Large bulbs such as daffodil, hyacinth, and tulip require deep planting; their pots should be deep. Smaller plants, including crocus, grape hyacinth, and striped squill, are shallowly planted, a good fit with wide, flat containers as deep as your hand. Later, you'll learn tips for choosing the right containers for your bulbs [see Selecting and Preparing Containers, pg. 47].

Bulbs are the perfect option for dressing up a stairway to an apartment or urban home's door. Use matching containers of red tulips (above) or orange-throated narcissus (left) greet visitors and add color even as they hide barren deciduous trees and shrubs.

The best container plantings crowd and layer bulbs to create massed color, using either a single species or mixing several bulbs with different colors and forms. You also can create successions of flowers, with early-, midseason-, and late-blooming varieties planted together to extend the bounty. Bulbs can be planted with annuals and perennials to create a living flower display.

Containers are a movable visual feast. They can follow the sun around a rooftop or balcony and can be clustered and arranged in groups to create pleasing changeable displays in many settings—entryways, patios, staircases, and window boxes.

While planning your bulb plantings, remember containers are a great way to beautify and soften the look and feel of your town or country home.

SPRING-BLOOMING BULBS

A h, the glory of spring bulbs! They likely are the very flowers you picture as you envision your landscape plantings, dream of cut flower arrangements, or flip through catalog pages with thoughts of the coming winter.

Despite their name, these bulbs are planted in autumn. They lie apparently at rest until stirred by spring's thaws and warmth. All at once, in what seems like a matter of days, they poke through the soil or snow with emerging flower spikes that soon open to bright, colorful blooms. For a time, while trees remain bare, they are the focal points of our gardens and landscapes, sporting little more than swelling buds that someday will open to flowers and new green leaves. Then, too quickly it seems, the bulbs' time passes, their flowers fade, and in a few months little remains to remind us of their presence other than withered brown foliage. We'll lift them gently from the soil, carefully clean and divide them, and put them in storage until autumn's cooling temperatures remind us that spring bulb planting time has come again.

Spring bulbs are great for growing along paths, fences, and borders. You can feature them in a formally designed island bed or let them reign in woodland or turf in drifts of yellow-headed daffodil or crimson hyacinth. Moist, shady areas provide the right environment for water-loving Louisiana iris, jack-in-the-pulpit, lily-of-the-valley, and trillium. Spring bulbs also are good choices to provide points of color in containers.

Some spring bulbs are suited for naturalizing—planting in beds or beneath turf-grass where they will return for many seasons—while others lose vigor, decline, or fail entirely in a single season. Climate conditions, especially the presence or absence of moisture during key portions of the bulbs' life cycle, determine whether they

(Left to right, both pgs.) Daffodil, hyacinth, tulip, Persian buttercup, crocus, and windflower are popular spring bulbs. (Above) A massed planting of daffodils in a meadow.

will naturalize. In some climates, lifting spring bulbs after they enter dormancy is essential before planting them again in autumn; some hybrids should be discarded after their blooms fade.

The spring bulbs are legion with species bearing unusual, thought-provoking names such as glory-of-the-snow, lily-of-the-valley, sentry-in-the-box, snowdrop, snowflake, spring starflower, and twelve-apostles as well as the familiar: bluebell, crocus, freesia, hyacinth, iris, tulip, and windflower, to name a few. They are favorites, destined to return at the same time each year when we most fervently desire their blooms.

Tulip is the queen of spring bulbs. Prized and bred for centuries, tulips have an astounding range of forms, flowers, color options, and appearances. Among those from which you will choose are early-, midseason-, and late-blooming varieties with single, double, fringed, or multiple flowers. There also are Darwin, Fosteriana, Gregii, lily-flowered, parrot, Rembrandt, triumph, viridiflora, and water-lily hybrids, cultivars, and species tulips, each with its own appealing features.

Flag iris, crocus, daffodil—and other narcissus—anemone, and hyacinth round out the finalists for the most popular spring bulbs. Like tulips, they also are offered in literally thousands of cultivars and hybrids, along with many hundreds of species—or wild—varieties.

Spring bulbs likely will be a highlight of your spring garden and landscape. They bloom reliably before most other plants and seeds germinate or begin to send up sprouts from their roots. Fresh shipments of new hybrids arrive in garden stores in early autumn, giving you the best choice at that time for beautifying your spring landscape. Unusual, rare, and specialty spring bulbs also are available directly from growers. If early color is your goal, plan on using spring bulbs to meet your objective and brighten your yard.

(Above) Tulips and forget-me-nots make good companion plantings and are attractive when mixed together in a garden bed. The low-growing forget-me-nots provide cover for the taller tulips' basal leaves and the bed's soil.

SUMMER-BLOOMING BULBS

The joy you derive from bulbs in spring continues with the flowering of summer bulbs. Whether you dress up a mixed-bed planting of shrubs with daylily, grow an eye-catching stand of lily and dahlia, or create a flowering border of gladiolus, summer bulbs are sure to draw attention to your landscape.

Summer bulbs usually are planted in spring, though they will overwinter successfully in mild-winter climates. Hardy summer bulbs are set into the garden soon after the soil becomes workable. For most tender varieties, though, the ground should be thoroughly warmed—at least 55°F (13°C)—before you plant them outdoors. Get a jump on the season by raising them in a cold frame or greenhouse protected from frost at night, or in a sunny indoor window.

Because many summer bulbs grow from rhizomes, tubers, and tuberous roots, they multiply quickly to form colonies well suited to landscape gardens. Daylily, iris, and lily-of-the-Nile will more than double in a season, offering you the chance to create new colonies [see Dividing Tubers and Rhizomes, pg. 80]. Some summer bulbs are of small stature and good for flowering ground covers; others grow tall and stately. A few species— caladium, elephant's-ear, and taro among them—are prized for distinctive, lush foliage, which adds depth and texture of near-tropical proportions.

Hardy summer bulbs include daylily, wild ginger, iris, lapeirousia, true lily, lords-and-ladies, montbretia, ornamental onion, star grass, windflower, and wood sorrel. The tender summer bulbs are more numerous; their ranks number some of the most beautiful summer flowers: tuberous begonia, caladium, calla lily, canna, dahlia, elephant's-ear, both common and fragrant gladiolus, summer hyacinth, wild hyacinth, lily-of the-Nile, pansy orchid, ranunculus, Mexican shellflower, Mexican tuberose, and some of the tropical lilies.

(Far left) A pathway edged with gladiolus. (Left) Cut gladiolus in an indoor arrangement. (Bottom, left to right) Oriental lily and dahlia.

(Opposite pg., clockwise from upper left) Flag iris, canna, freesia, and tuberous begonia.

Two summer bulbs are best loved, if the number planted each year is any guide: lily and gladiolus. Like favorite spring bulbs, many hybrids and cultivars of these have been bred by growers, and new selections are added to the old favorites offered every year. Both include cultivars that are tall and striking.

Lilies grow from true bulbs with sword-shaped leaves that radiate from a central stem topped with a circle of large, trumpet, nodding, or bowl-shaped flowers. Earliest blooming of the lilies are the Asiatic, which flower in early summer, followed by the mid-summer-flowering trumpet and Aurelian lilies, then by the Oriental hybrids in late summer into autumn. A number of other plants bear lily-shaped flowers but are classified separately from true lily, including daylily and lily-of-the-Nile.

Gladiolus, or sword lily, actually is a member of the iris family that grows from corms buried 4–6 in. (10–15 cm) deep in the soil. Its colorful flower spikes with tiers of deep-throated flowers appear separate from its foliage, which is long and tapered with highly visible veins. There are short, midsize, and tall hybrids in a range of pastel, primary, and multihued colors.

In the 1920s, dahlia was among the most popular of the summer flowers; its popularity waned later in the century but recently was revived as growers released more varied and disease-resistant hybrid cultivars.

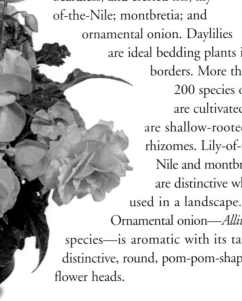

Among other summer bulb favorites are daylily; bearded, beardless, and crested iris; lily-of-the-Nile; montbretia; and ornamental onion. Daylilies are ideal bedding plants in borders. More than 200 species of iris are cultivated; all are shallow-rooted rhizomes. Lily-of-the-Nile and montbretia are distinctive when used in a landscape. Ornamental onion—*Allium* species—is aromatic with its tall, distinctive, round, pom-pom-shaped flower heads.

AUTUMN BLOOMING BULBS

(Above) Cyclamen is an excellent choice for both outdoor plantings and indoor containers. (Right) Some autumn crocus cultivars have characteristics of true crocus though they are entirely different plants; others are simply crocus that bud and bloom in autumn.

Autumn usually signals the start of a time of rest in a garden whose season of flowering is ended. Fortunately, autumn-blooming bulbs stand ready with colorful flowers that fit the season and fill the empty spaces in beds where our annual flowers and spring bulbs once bloomed.

Autumn-blooming bulbs arrive at the garden store and nursery in spring, along with summer bulbs. Plant them in spring after the soil has warmed. Marking their planting site will help you locate them and avoid overplanting with perennial flowers and shrubs. A cane marker is sturdy and easily seen, yet disappears amid other foliage and flowers.

Autumn bloomers can be used throughout the landscape. Short species are best as a border edging, while tall varieties provide a surprise focal point. Some of the tallest autumn bulb plants provide quite a show with blooms that stand high atop barren stalks long after their foliage has disappeared.

Autumn bulbs include hardy begonia, two varieties of autumn crocus—*Colchicum* and *Crocus* frequently are called by the same common name—autumn cyclamen, lily-of-the-field, lords-and-ladies, naked-lady, rain lily, and autumn snowflake. Hardy begonia is actually a half-hardy perennial that tolerates climates with winter temperatures down to about 0°F (-18°C). In areas with colder winters, hardy begonias should be lifted in late autumn and their tubers stored in a cold, dry spot. They bloom from midsummer through late autumn.

True autumn crocus flowers resemble those of spring crocus, while the colchicum varieties have wider leaves and bear their larger, star-shaped flowers in basketball-sized clusters containing as many as 25 blooms or more. Both bloom from late summer to midautumn.

Autumn cyclamen flowers are commonly deep pink, rarely white, and the plant sprouts wide, toothed leaves similar to maple or ivy. Look for the first blooms in late summer.

Lords-and-ladies, or *Arum,* are shade-loving tubers related to jack-in-the-pulpit. Their oval leaves mask stout shoots bearing colorful clusters of surprising berrylike fruit in autumn that began with calla-like blossoms in spring.

Autumn lilies include rain lily and naked-lady, which flowers in autumn after its foliage fades in midsummer.

As you begin your quest for the perfect bulb garden, you'll have to make several fundamental choices. First, will you devote an entire bed to bulbs, or will you use them selectively in your garden? Second, will your landscape plantings be formal or informal? The answer to these questions will guide your decisions as you plan your plantings, select bulbs, and create your garden.

If you choose to plant a special bulb garden, the size of your project will be determined by the boundaries of the bed, and many other decisions quickly will fall into place. If, on the other hand, you decide to use bulbs as accents to your landscape, or to place a container or two of bulbs on a deck, you'll want to coordinate them with their surroundings.

The two dominant garden forms are formal and informal—sometimes called natural—landscapes. The origin of formal gardens stems from landscapes of the Middle Ages, including those found in monasteries, palaces, and cloisters of Europe and the Mideast. Crusaders who were exposed to Holy Land gardens featuring geometric patterns took the concept back to Europe with them. Similar gardens designed with repeated, symmetrical elements were soon seen throughout France, Italy, and Spain.

Trade with the Orient beginning in the 1700s introduced to Europe a competing design concept frequently seen in Chinese and Japanese gardens—symbolic naturalism. While gardens following this approach appear as natural as true wild settings, they actually have underlying design principles based on fluid, sinuous forms, circles, and ovals to unify their elements. Over time, this approach has become popular, and bulb gardens abound with naturalized beds of crocus, daffodil, hyacinth, and tulip planted in drifts along hillsides and beneath tree bowers.

You may be drawn to either formal beds or natural ones, and your landscape likely can match your evolving vision. Bulb plantings that you admire in another gardener's yard often contain individual elements suited to a variety of landscape settings. Modify them to enhance your garden or use them to trigger new ideas that you can apply. Always keep in mind the size of your site and your choice of style as you seek inspiration in the media or in public gardens, and be encouraged by the endless possibilities.

FORMAL AND INFORMAL GARDENS

Whether you plant your bulbs in formal patterns (far left) or allow them to naturalize in grass under a glade of trees (lower right), a colorful display results when they bloom. Planters (lower left) and baskets (below) are good accents for use in small-space gardens. Move them indoors to dress up a table in your home.

(Following page) A formal mixed planting features annual and perennial flowers, tulips, and hedge borders of green shrubs.

Your mental picture of your garden landscape is probably one of a completed bulb planting in glorious bloom. Before your dream can become reality, however, some care and planning are necessary when choosing the site, laying out your garden, selecting the bulbs, and obtaining all the advice, tools, and materials you'll need. The Bulb Garden Checklist provides a useful overview of all the necessary steps to creating a bulb garden, from concept to reality. Later in the book, you'll learn how to implement the important decisions that you make now.

You'll start by finding your plant hardiness zone, judging the climatic conditions your bulbs will face, and learning how your landscape may have features different from those of other garden sites in your area. Armed with that knowledge, you'll look at your site again, determining its sun exposure, shade conditions, and the nature and fertility of your soil.

Make choices, plan, and pick a site as you decide its form and function— two keys to every successful landscape

Bulb Garden Checklist

Next, you'll gain inspiration from examples of bulb gardens found in this and other books, periodicals, and through electronic information resources. You'll review your objectives and goals, weighing them against any requirements your site or situation imposes, and you'll decide which garden style to use for your bulb planting.

The next step, before beginning to select bulbs and preparing your design, is to evaluate how large your bulb garden should be, from a container garden on your porch to a landscape filled with naturalized bulbs. You'll decide the scope and scale of your project, setting guidelines in place that will help you decide how many bulbs to purchase and plant.

Finally, you'll plan the garden itself, using design principles based on repeating geometric forms, color combinations, and flower forms. Insight into how beds and borders are planned will help you bring floral beauty to your yard.

Before your dreams can be fulfilled and you can have a glorious garden filled with dahlias, some careful planning will save effort and assure that you will have the best possible results.

Also in this chapter, you'll be given tips to find the best information sources, from some literally at your fingertips or in your hometown to those found half a world away. The special tools and materials you'll need to garden with bulbs are itemized, so you will have them ready when you begin your project.

CHOOSING A SITE

Bulbs have a place in every garden: in containers and window boxes, for small-space gardens, in island beds, in borders, as edges to paths and fences, to divide and augment plantings of flowering shrubs, as a necklace around the base of a tree, and in a hundred other places. Choosing a site for planting a bulb garden usually is an easy task.

Start by determining the conditions in your garden and which bulbs will perform best. Bulb species are native to varied lands that experience a range of climate conditions. The U.S. Department of Agriculture (USDA) has divided the world into 11 zones according to the average lowest temperatures they experience [see USDA Plant Hardiness Zones Around the World, pg. 132]. Look at the map for your region, note its color on the legend, and determine your zone. Bulbs are listed in most references with notes about the coldest plant hardiness zone in which they will grow.

Next, consider your climate. Your garden likely has one of three climates: cold, freezing winters and moist, warm summers; mild, wet winters and hot, dry summers; or generally mild winters with humid, wet summers. There are bulbs that are well-suited to each of these climate conditions.

Two popular sites frequently selected for bulb plantings are corner beds (below) and borders (bottom). Remember that an island bed in a lawn can also be a dramatic way to showcase your colorful bulbs in a landscape.

Your site also may be affected by microclimates: wind and sun exposure, slopes and elevation, and nearby structures that limit sunlight or reflect heat. Microclimate conditions can cause your plant hardiness zone to differ from your neighbors. Ask experienced staff at your garden store, nursery, or USDA or Agriculture Canada extension for advice about conditions in your area.

Note how much sunlight the area you're considering receives at various times of the day. Do trees and structures cast shade, and is it full shade or filtered? Will the situation change when trees and shrubs lose their leaves? Some bulbs need full sunlight to grow well, while others thrive in shade.

Will your site host spring or summer bulbs, and will you plant them amid other annual and perennial flowers, or woody shrubs and ground covers? What nutrition, watering, and other care needs do your perennials, shrubs, and trees require, and will they be disturbed when you lift your tulips, daffodils, and other bulbs after they bloom?

What is the condition of the soil? Has the bed been used to grow other plants, lain fallow for a few years, or was the site disturbed when your home was constructed? Is the soil dense and compacted, or loose and sandy? Will you need to add fertilizers and amendments to bolster its nutrients and correct its acid-alkaline balance, or pH?

Ask these questions to determine the bulbs you plant and the look of your garden.

As you plan your bulb garden, keep in mind practical needs, such as including low-voltage pathway lighting for safety.

ESTABLISHING OBJECTIVES AND PURPOSE

Now is a good time to reflect on your goals and objectives for your bulb plantings. While your overall purpose may be to beautify your landscape in the spring before trees bud with new leaves and annual flowers begin to bloom, you may have other considerations worth exploring.

If you garden indoors, in a small space such as a patio, deck, or courtyard, or simply have a small area to devote to bulbs, you should plan carefully to achieve the effect you desire. Container gardens and structured landscapes are good spots for geometric groupings of containers or plantings set off by raised beds or other well-defined edges. Consider strong, contrasting color palettes bordered with complementary colors.

In larger settings, you may wish to create a showcase in a bed or border devoted to your bulbs, or you might prefer flowing naturalized plantings that duplicate the look of an informal garden. As you plan, try to picture your site with various plantings, gathering ideas from books, periodicals, television programs, or other media.

Your garden may suggest a plan by its shape, layout, structures, or overall design. Paths, for instance, may need border plantings to line their edges, or a glade of silver birch may call for daffodils in a faux meadow. Your bulb planting will best fit your site when it matches and integrates with the setting; choose colors, plants, and layouts that are rustic, casual, structured, or formal depending on your home's architectural style.

Also consider your secondary objectives: Should the bulbs hide raw soil before a deciduous ground cover develops leaves in spring? Has water remained standing on the site in the past, creating a perfect locale for moisture-loving bulbs such as flag iris? Will your tall plantings of dahlia and gladiolus mask a fence, water spigot, or electrical fixture? All of these considerations may shape your decisions as you plan your bulb garden.

The hard edges of a herringbone brick path and its low formal hedges can be softened by using tall bulbs to create a casual and undulating form that accents the shrubs that frame it.

SCALE AND PLANNING

Scope and scale are flip sides of the same coin. Scope roughly translates to your estimate of the degree of your involvement and the commitment needed to accomplish your goals, while scale measures the size and extent of the plantings you see in your mind's eye.

If you have a busy schedule and limited leisure time, you should plan a garden that fits with your lifestyle: a few containers of colorful bulbs to feature on the steps of your home's entry, a trim line of crocus to line a walk, or a single island bed in the middle of your front lawn.

If, on the other hand, you have more leisure time to spend in the garden, larger bulb plantings might be in order. Most bulbs require major care twice per season, at planting and when lifting them after bloom, so factor their needs into your schedule. The grand bulb plantings you so admire in a public garden probably took a staff of several gardeners a week or more to complete. It's a day's considerable effort to plant a few hundred tulips and daffodils, and maybe two more to lift and prepare them for winter storage. Still, if your objective is a striking springtime appearance for your home and your love of gardening supports your ambition, plan as large a bulb garden as befits your landscape.

Bulb gardens can be any size, from mixed landscape plantings (below) to a solitary hyacinth bulb forced in a decorative hyacinth glass well-suited to a desk (right).

You also can tackle plans with larger scope by taking advantage of the right planting techniques, using labor-saving equipment, and enlisting the assistance of helpers. You might consider acquiring an electric soil auger for your cordless drill to simplify and speed planting, for instance, or seek out a landscape garden contractor for a few days to install your beds.

Remember that naturalized plantings of hardy species that reliably repeat their blooms naturally become more abundant as the seasons pass. Species tulips and daffodils, for instance, seldom require the degree of care necessary for single-season, formal plantings. Leave them to care for themselves if your climate supports such bulbs.

Once you have decided your commitment and have planned accordingly, you will be able to choose the scale of your bulb planting. Look anew at your site in light of your recent thoughts and decisions. Use a garden hose or colored yarn to help you visualize the edges of the future bed. Adjust the size and shape of the planting until it both fits the site and accommodates any nearby structures, trees, or fences. When it is right, use wooden stakes to mark the placement and perimeter of the bed.

The way you arrange bubs within your plantings creates order and symmetry in your garden and landscape. Massed bulbs—tightly clustered groups of a single species—are most attractive when they are planted in a geometric pattern. This is true for multiple bulb plantings as well. Even gardens that appear randomly arranged usually are based on geometric design elements—circles and ovals, squares and rectangles, triangles, plus lines or rows—which frequently are overlapped or truncated, giving the plantings their casual appearance.

Bulb species also can be interspersed, either with another bulb or with an annual or perennial flower such as forget-me-not. This creates a high-low pattern that adds texture to the plantings. For best results when interspersing two or more species, choose colors that are pleasing together such as white and blue, or orange and yellow, and plants with growth habits that complement one another. The cone-shaped flower form of hyacinth, for example, is attractive when inset with tall and dainty English or Spanish bluebells.

Plan your arrangement of species from the center of the bed to its edges—or from the back of a border to its front—placing the tallest bulbs in the middle or back. As you move toward the edge, step down in height so that the outside flowers mask the foliage of the interior bulbs while allowing their blooms to be seen. The shorter species, such as grape hyacinth and crocus, are easily visible along the margins. Choose varieties with similar blooming times for a striking spectacle, or those that bloom in sequence to sustain the display [see Bloom Seasons of Common Bulbs, pg. 24].

When choosing bulbs, consider foliage texture as well as blooms, especially when planting summer and autumn bulbs. You might want to make a bold statement with a bulb prized primarily for its distinctive foliage, such as elephant's-ear or caladium, or to create a lush tropical feel with canna or woodlily. Lily-of-the-Nile and dahlia have sustained blooms once they flower, and their lush foliage is attractive long before the color emerges.

FORM AND DESIGN

Enhance existing garden elements with bulbs. This formal reflecting pool found in Buchart Gardens in Victoria, B.C. is accented with pink fringed tulips, yellow Siberian wallflowers planted with blue bugloss, and white forget-me-nots.

SOURCES OF BULBS AND RESOURCES FOR INFORMATION

(Below) A wealth of resources are available for obtaining information about bulbs, their planting, and care. Start at your local garden center or nursery, which has experienced staff ready to answer your questions and give helpful tips.

(Right) Catalogs, periodicals, and garden newsletters highlight new plants and provide grower sources.

Information about bulbs and how to acquire or plant them is easy to come by. It's as near as the staff of your garden retailer; shared at public gardens and arboretums; dispensed from governmental agencies such as the USDA and Agriculture Canada; offered through bulb-specific and general gardening organizations; included in packaged bulbs obtained from direct retailers and garden centers; printed in books, periodicals, and catalogs; taught in adult extension classes; and also is available through many different electronic resources and media outlets.

Your local nursery, garden center, or home store is the best starting point for region-specific advice about which varieties to plant, the care they will need, and special guidance for beginning gardeners. Managers and staff at most garden stores have experience in the growing of bulbs, and they stock the most popular varieties grown in your area.

A public garden or arboretum is your next stop. Helpful docents and staff garden specialists can give you information about the species they grow, will help identify diseases or pests troubling your plants, and will refer you to garden experts.

For the best technical advice about bulbs, consult a university, the USDA, or an Agriculture Canada extension office in your area. Local extension agents have academic and practical experience, plus resources they can share containing specialty knowledge about specific disease, pest, and culture situations that you may encounter in your garden. They also can provide you with numerous pamphlets and other publications, including those containing general gardening information, sources of bulbs, and plant recommendations suited for your climate, soil, and growing conditions.

You also can obtain detailed advice about how to grow various flowering bulbs from national organizations devoted to daffodil, dahlia, iris, and lily [see On-Line Index, pg. 134]. Often, these are the best sources to learn about recent bulb introductions.

Another good source of data about bulbs is often packaged with them. You can obtain bulbs from specialists and ultra-specialists, who may offer either a single bulb species in many different cultivars or can provide several different species; general bulb suppliers, who grow a wide range of bulbous plants; or general garden retailers, who offer only the most popular bulbs. Always remember to adapt any information included with bulbs obtained directly from the grower to suit your climate, plant hardiness zone, and local conditions.

Easy-to-access electronic resources provide descriptions of unusual bulbs and other useful information directly from experts who grow or market the bulbs.

TOOLS AND MATERIALS

Bulbs require fewer specialized tools for planting and care than do many other landscape plants. Similarly, they will grow in a wide range of soils and usually need only average fertility. Consider obtaining these specialty items as you prepare to plant and care for bulbs:

- **Adjustable rake**. Variable tine-width settings allow you to spread or narrow the prongs when raking between rows of plants.
- **Bedding fork**. Square-tined forks penetrate deeply and lift bulbs from beneath.
- **Bulb planter**. Hollow metal tool for cutting and removing turf and soil for bulb planting.
- **Combination hoe**. With a pointed blade on one side, tined fork on the other, cultivates soil around bulbs.
- **Dibber**. Pointed, solid metal tool for poking planting holes for bulbs. May compact dense soils.
- **Gloves**. Leather or reinforced canvas protects hands from abrasion when planting and lifting.
- **Grub knife**. Multipurpose knife with one serrated and one smooth edge used to divide roots.
- **Planting fertilizer**. Organic or synthetic fertilizer of 0–10–10 formulation used beneath bulb plantings.
- **Shovel**. Square or round points facilitate penetration and turnover when loosening soil in garden beds.

Turn to your local bookstore or public library for a variety of publications about bulbs, photographs of the varieties, and information about culture and care, or turn to the specific bulb information included in this book [see Encyclopedia of Bulbous Plants, pg. 95].

Many monthly periodicals on gardening frequently include articles about bulbs that are timed to appear when either spring or summer bulbs first appear in nurseries, garden centers, and catalogs.

Adult education classes and electronic information sources also have become popular resources for information about many bulbous plants. The curricula of night classes held at high schools and many communitity colleges now include gardening instruction taught by knowledgeable instructors. Home computers connected to electronic information resources as well as broadcast and cable television programs provide inspiration, facts, and resources for acquiring bulbs for direct delivery. Whenever you use information provided by the media or electronic sources, remember to tailor the advice to fit your climate, plant hardiness zone, and locale. Nearly everwhere you look, you'll find expert, practical advice and assistance for planning, planting, and growing your bulb garden.

BULB PLANNING FLOWCHART

A flowchart is a planning tool that allows you to scan the important questions that need to be answered as you plan your garden. In landscaping, as in most other projects, there is a sequence in which tasks should be done. By planning an orderly flow of steps and arranging for tools and materials to be on site when needed, you can reduce wasted time and duplicated effort. As you go through the following questions you can also develop a timetable for your garden project.

1 **Site Choice Questions:**
In what USDA plant hardiness zone is your garden located? Is it subject to microclimates caused by elevation, slope, sun and wind exposure, or nearby structures? How does your climate affect your plans? Is your soil loose and well-drained, or compacted? Will you perform a soil test for nutrients and acid-alkaline balance? What amendments and fertilizers are needed? Will you need new garden features, structures, or paths? What is the overall size of your plantings? Will you plant spring-, summer-, or autumn-blooming bulbs?

UNDERSTANDING YOUR SITE

DETERMINING GOALS

2 **Goal Questions:**
What use is ideal for your site? What objective will your plantings accomplish? How will the garden be used, and by whom? What feature, bed, or border will be the landscape's focal point? What public gardens or arboretums are available as information or idea resources? Does your planned garden fit your home and its surroundings? What are your resources, skills, and budget? What is your schedule for completing the project? Will you implement your plan in stages or all at once?

CHOOSING SITE IMPROVEMENTS

3 **Scale Questions:**
How large is the site, and how is it naturally divided? What is the central theme for each area? What priorities do you have for each aspect of the project? Has your site previously been used for plantings? What steps are necessary to make your garden suitable for bulbs? Will you install garden systems—electric, plumbing, lighting—or add features? Is help readily available, or will you seek the aid of a professional? How long will it take to assemble tools and equipment and to install the garden? How much time is available for maintenance and care?

4 Bulb Selection Questions:

Will you plant your bulbs for spring, summer, autumn, or winter bloom? Does each bulb fit your site and soil conditions? Are the bulbs adapted to your climate, or will they require post-bloom lifting, curing, and storage? Are you available for both planting and follow-up care? Does your local garden retailer stock quality bulbs, or will you obtain them from a direct retailer or specialist? Are you familiar with the planting timing and needs of each bulb? What blooms and foliage patterns fit your garden plan? What color scheme have you picked? Will the bulbs bloom together or follow each other in succession? Will the bulbs require chilling or storage prior to planting? Will you force bulbs during winter and spring to enjoy their bloom indoors and out of season?

PREPARING TO PURCHASE BULBS

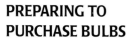

5 Preparation Questions:

Do you have trees, shrubs, or other plants and structures to be removed? Will you plant in lawn or turfgrass? When will you build planter boxes, obtain containers, and install garden features or systems? When will you prepare soil for planting by amending and fertilizing the site? What tools, equipment, and materials will you require? How long will each task take? Is the weather right for planting? Is your garden plan complete, and have you assembled all the bulbs you'll need to complete the planting? If you pot in containers, where will you work? Do you have a storage site for the planted containers that is suitable to each bulbs' needs?

ORGANIZING TIME, TOOLS, AND TASKS

FINDING HELP AND INFORMATION

6 Resource and Aid Questions:

What steps will you do yourself? Will you seek professional aid or other helpers? Where can you get information on your local climate, conditions, and the best bulbs for your region? Where will you gain the knowledge for building projects? Are there specialists or retail staff that can give you advice on building and gardening projects? What are your community resources, such as arboretums, public gardens, libraries, educational programs, and extension offices? Do you have access to electronic information sources? What periodicals should you read? Are there media programs that permit call-in questions that could help you make choices?

U nderstanding the superficially similar though different bulbous plants usually loosely referred to as spring, summer, autumn, and winter bulbs is a helpful beginning to deciding which species you should plant in your garden or landscape.

You'll discover in this chapter that bulbs are specially adapted to grow in specific climates, including those with dry summers and wet winters; others with warm, wet summers and cool, dry winters; and still others with mild winters and hot summers punctuated by intermittent rains. Bulbs, you'll find, require care when they're planted in hardiness zones that are different from their native lands. You'll also learn about the bulb's life cycle and when many common bulb species flower.

Next, you'll examine the difference between spring bulbs, planted in autumn for bloom the following year, and summer, autumn, and winter bulbs, planted in spring after cold weather has passed. As you plan your layered and mixed-species plantings, you'll consult the convenient Planting Depth Chart.

Whether you plan just a few container plantings or an elaborate landscape, here you will find all the information you need to create a colorful display. Small-space gardeners will discover suggestions on how to arrange containers as well as instructions for building an attractive window box suitable for spring bulb plantings in the autumn, and for planting summer bulbs and annual and perennial flowers in the summer. Landscape gardeners will find guidelines to plan beds and borders using formal plans and naturalized beds filled with beautiful, blooming bulbs. You'll also learn how to use a color wheel to create eye-catching plantings, create drifts of bulbs, and add interest by varying heights.

Finally, you'll consider garden structures and systems to make your gardening easier and enhance the look of your beds and borders. We'll show you how to construct a natural-looking raised bed, using native stone as an edging material; how to test your soil for its nutrients, texture, and acidity to suit your bulbs' needs; and how to amend and improve your soil.

Learn bulb basics and plan your garden, then install features to add beauty and make its care quick and easy

Planning and Preparing Bulb Gardens

As you plan for all of the beauty of colorful spring bulbs peeking through a bower of raining flower petals, take the time to gather your ideas and find examples of gardens to guide you by looking in periodicals and books.

BULB BASICS

The main difference between bulbs and other growing plants has to do with their root systems. Trees, shrubs, grasses, and flowers generally have permanent roots that extend down into the soil from a trunk or stalk. Experiencing heat and drought, they wilt and require care to sustain them. Bulbous plants, which store water and nutrients in swollen structures partially buried or beneath the soil, are able to survive drought by becoming dormant during seasonal periods of drought.

Bulbous plants comprise their own specialized group from among many different plant types, but it's convenient to divide them into four general classes by bloom season: spring, summer, autumn, and tropical or evergreen bulbs [see Classification of Bulbous Plants, pg. 26]. While some bulbs straddle more than one of these largely artificial classes, most fit into one category.

Native habitats of bulbs range from frosty and near-polar, as for spring crocus (above), to the tropics and subtropics, that of florist's amaryllis (right), and moist-winter, arid-summer climates, as for wandflower.

Spring bulbs mostly are native to areas with hot, dry summers and cool or cold, wet winters. Nearly dormant in summer, they sprout roots and buds in winter, developing foliage and flowers in spring. They include daffodil and other narcissus, crocus, some fritillary, hyacinth, iris, ornamental onion, and tulip.

Most summer bulbs originate in regions with climates of warm, rainy summers and cool, dry winters. Near-dormant in winter, they become active in spring and bloom in mid-summer. Caladium, canna, dahlia, daylily, gladiolus, and lily are popular summer-flowering bulbs.

Autumn bulbs are adapted to climates with hot, dry summers, moist autumns, and mild to cool, dry winters. Examples include hardy begonia, caladium, autumn-blooming crocus, meadow saffron, and sternbergia.

Many evergreen bulbs live in areas with intermittent rains and mild temperatures; others are found in tropical locales with occasional dry periods. They retain year-round foliage and bloom when moisture is abundant. Examples include amaryllis, tuberous begonia, perennial ginger, and lily-of-the-Nile.

BLOOM SEASONS OF COMMON BULBS

Many gardeners choose bulbs to create beautiful color displays in their flower beds. While the specific bloom time varies by climate and the manner in which the bulbs were stored prior to planting, you can plan bulb gardens of great beauty by choosing from among these common bulbs according to nature's rhythm and cycles:

Early spring: *Anemone blanda*, crocus hybrids, glory-of-the-snow, reticulated iris, narcissus (early varieties), snowdrop, striped squill, tulip (early varieties and species), windflower, and winter aconite.

Spring: Daffodil, fritillary, hyacinth, grape hyacinth, Dutch iris, lily-of-the-valley, narcissus (late varieties), scilla (early varieties), spring snowflake, squill, starflower, and tulip (Darwin and Mendel hybrids).
Late spring: English bluebell, bearded iris, foxtail lily, scilla (late varieties), Spanish bluebell, star-of-Bethlehem, and tulip (parrot).
Summer: Amaryllis, anemone, tuberous begonia, caladium, canna, dahlia, daylily, elephant's-ear, gladiolus, summer hyacinth, lily, torch lily, lycoris, montbretia, ranunculus, tuberose, and wood sorrel.

Autumn: Hardy begonia, caladium, autumn crocus, cyclamen, meadow saffron, and sternbergia.
Indoor Forcing: Amaryllis, crocus, cyclamen, daffodil, freesia, Dutch and reticulated iris, hyacinth, grape hyacinth, lily-of-the-valley, narcissus (paperwhite, miniatures), and wood sorrel.
Tropical and Evergreen: Miniature amaryllis, tuberous begonia, caladium, calla, canna, clivia, cyclamen, elephant's-ear, ginger, gloxinia, woodlily, spider lily, tuber nasturtium, ornamental onion, nut orchid, taro, wood sorrel, and Persian violet.

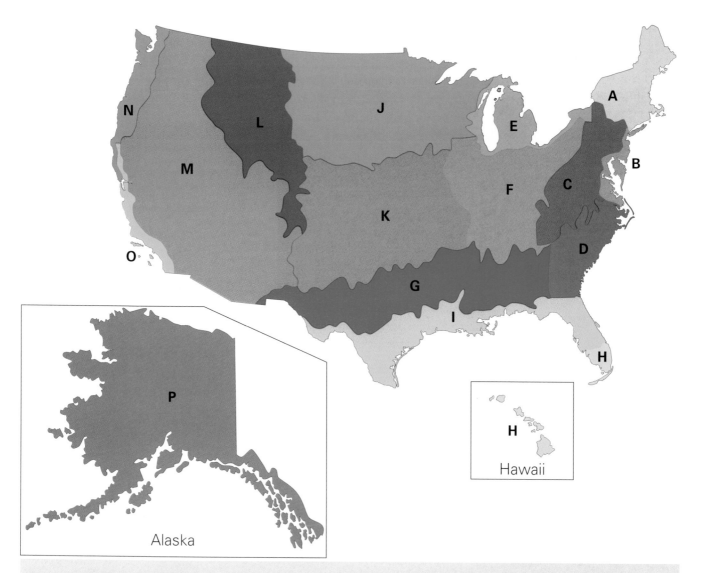

BULB PLANTING REGIONS

A. New England—USDA Plant Hardiness Zones 3, 4, 5. Optimum planting time: September 15–November 15.

B. Mid-Atlantic Coast—USDA Plant Hardiness Zones 6, 7, 8. Optimum planting time: October 1–November 30.

C. Appalachia—USDA Plant Hardiness Zones 5, 6. Optimum planting time: September 15–November 30.

D. South Atlantic Coast—USDA Plant Hardiness Zones 7, 8. Optimum planting time: October 15–December 15.

E. Great Lakes—USDA Plant Hardiness Zones 5, 6, 7. Optimum planting time: September 15–November 15.

F. East Central—USDA Plant Hardiness Zones 5, 6, 7. Optimum planting time: October 1–November 30.

G. South Central—USDA Plant Hardiness Zones 7, 8. Optimum planting time: October 15–December 15.

H. Tropical—USDA Zone 10. Optimum planting time: December 1–January 15.

I. Gulf Coast—USDA Plant Hardiness Zones 8, 9. Optimum planting time: October 1–December 31.

J. North Central—USDA Plant Hardiness Zones 3, 4, 5. Optimum planting time: September 15–November 1.

K. Central Great Plains—USDA Plant Hardiness Zones 5, 6. Optimum planting time: September 30–November 30.

L. Rocky Mountains—USDA Plant Hardiness Zones 2, 3, 4. Optimum planting time: September 15–November 1.

M. Arid West—USDA Plant Hardiness Zones 5, 6, 7. Optimum planting time: September 30–November 30.

N. North Pacific Coast—USDA Zone 8. Optimum planting time: October 1–November 30.

O. South Pacific Coast—USDA Plant Hardiness Zones 9, 10. Optimum planting time: August 15–December 15 (baboon flower, flame freesia, freesia, bearded iris, corn lily, ornamental onion, squill, wandflower, wood sorrel); August 15–January 31 (bluebell, Persian buttercup (ranunculus), daffodil, grape hyacinth, Dutch iris, lily, windflower).

P. Alaska—USDA Plant Hardiness Zones 1–7. Optimum planting time: September 15–October 15.

Source: Netherlands Flower Bulb Information Center

CLASSIFICATION OF BULBOUS PLANTS

The plants generally referred to as bulbs have swollen, specialized roots, stems, or modified leaves that store nascent buds, moisture, and nutrients beneath the ground. Underground storage protects and allows them to become dormant— sacrifice their foliage when drought, extreme heat, or cold conditions settle in to stay —then flourish again when growing conditions become favorable.

There are five broad horticultural categories of bulbous plants: true bulbs, corms, rhizomes, tubers, and tuberous roots.

- **True Bulb**—A platelike base of modified stem tissue with attached, scalelike storage leaves and a central growth bud, often complete with an embryonic bloom, stem, and leaves. Bulbs bear concentric rings if cut parallel to the base plate. They regenerate fully each year, often forming small offsets called "bulblets" along their basal plate, or forming seed or "bulbils" at either the site of their former flowers or, in the case of some lilies, at their axils—the junctions of stems and leaves.

- **Corm**—A swollen, underground stem atop a platelike base with one or more growth buds, usually bearing a flaky, dry, skinlike covering that preserves moisture. Corms appear solid, lacking visible structures inside. They are depleted and wither as the plants grow, and a new corm forms on top of the old. Offspring—called "cormels"—form around the base of the new corm, taking 2–4 years to flower if detached and raised separately.

- **Rhizome**—A modified thickened stem that lies horizontally atop the soil, partially beneath, or completely underground, bearing scalelike leaves with nascent buds at each axil. Rhizomes branch outward to form new plants, each with independent roots and growth buds, as the parent root withers and dries.

- **Tuber**—Depending on species, either modified stems or roots lacking internal structures, with minuscule surface scales bearing eyes, or growth buds along its surface. Tubers usually appear solid when cut. Like corms, many species of tuber shrivel as the plants grow and nutrients stored within are consumed; simultaneously, they multiply by division to form new tubers. Others renew and enlarge their tuber each season.

- **Tuberous Root**—Engorged, fibrous, modified roots surround a crown—the junction of the stem with the root—bearing growth buds on the crown. True roots emerge from the tuberous root, and stems, leaves, and flowers sprout from the crown. Over time, multiple crowns emerge from the expanding mass of tuberous roots, creating offspring plants.

Most bulbous plants are petaloid monocotyledons—meaning they sprout a single leaf as their seeds germinate and they have petaled flowers. The rest are dicotyledons: tuberous-rooted anenomes, cyclamen, eranthis, a few ranunculus, and wood sorrel. They are specialized members of plant families that include both annual and perennial species.

True bulbs, such as tulip (top), have an onionskin-like tunic that surrounds the bulb and helps prevent it from drying. Crocus, a corm (above), also has a tunic. Its interior differs from true bulbs by being solid and uniform, while bulbs have an embryonic plant at the center of concentric spheres of fleshy tissue.

LIFE CYCLES OF BULBS

Bulbous plants generally spend part of the year inactive in a dormantlike state. For evergreen bulbs, this is merely a period of slowed growth, and some tropicals provide year-round, lush-green foliage. For most bulbs, however, resting starts with the onset of dry weather. Foliage yellows, withers, then turns brown. After a month or two, the bulb rests in the soil, awaiting rain.

The onset of rain—or irrigation—causes a stirring within the bulb. As soil moisture penetrates the plant's tissue, it begins to put down roots. In cold-winter areas, freezing may interrupt this root growth, which begins again as temperatures moderate. When conditions are optimal a foliage shoot emerges from the bulb, breaking the soil. In a remarkably short time—sometimes only a few weeks—leaves, stem, bud, and bloom appear. This growth spurt is fueled by the nutrients stored within the bulb. As the bulb is depleted, it either withers entirely, as in the case of corms and some tubers, or shrinks in size. Simultaneously, new offsets are formed, and seeds or bulbils form.

Following bloom, the foliage supplies nutrients for the next year's bulbs. Offsets swell in size, beginning their independent growth from the parent bulb. When the cycle is complete, the bulb rests until new rains fall.

The most common bulbs generally belong to three families—amaryllis (AMARYLLIDACEAE), iris (IRIDACEAE), and lily (LILIACEAE)—and members of those widespread families can be found in virtually every geographic region except the poles. Fully a third of all the genera containing bulbous plants are represented in South Africa. Growers have yet to explore all of the possible disease- and pest-resistant varieties, vibrant colors, and enticing scents of bulbs as they continue to hybridize wild species and create new cultivars.

Some popular genera, including tulip and narcissus, have been divided further into formal horticultural classifications, termed divisions:

- **Narcissus divisions:** (1) trumpet, (2) large-cupped, (3) small-cupped, (4) double, (5) Triandrus, (6) Cyclamineus, (7) Jonquilla (8) Tazetta, (9) Poeticus, (10) species and wild forms, (11) split-corona, and (12) other narcissus.
- **Tulip divisions:** (1) single early, (2) double early, (3) triumph, (4) Darwin hybrid, (5) single late (Darwin and cottage), (6) lily-flowered, (7) fringed, (8) veridiflora, (9) Rembrandt, (10) parrot, (11) double late (peony-flowered), (12) Kaufmanniana hybrids, (13) Fosterana hybrids, (14) Greigii hybrids, and (15) other species, varieties, and hybrids.

Bulbs vary according to their botanic classification and structural form. True bulbs hold a complete plant within them—roots, stems, leaves, and embryonic flowers—while the other bulb categories largely contain differentiated cells that will give rise to the mature plant's parts clustered in growing points.

Bulbs have developed life cycles that permit them to grow and bloom under a wide range of conditions. Because of their diverse origins, there are bulbs suited to every garden, purpose, climate, and soil. Each bulbous plant you'll grow in your garden or indoors is fully adapted to a specific climate somewhere in the wild. Hardy bulbs capable of weathering the cold-winter climates are found in their native mountains of China, Japan, Russia, and Turkey. Tender bulbs hail from central Asia, South Africa, Mediterranean climates such as Northern Africa and southern Europe. Tropical species require mild weather for planting outdoors and will thrive indoors provided they receive adequate light and moisture.

Identifying a specific bulb for planting in your garden begins by knowing its two names: the common name, such as jonquil, and the scientific one—usually in Latin or latinized Greek and standardized by botanists throughout the world—such as *Narcissus jonquilla*. The main scientific name consists of two words, the plant's genus followed by the species.

Common names, while colorful and useful, vary by region and locale, often are used for plants of different species, and frequently change over time as horticulturists reclassify plants. To identify a specific cultivar, its variety name appears in single quotes after the scientific names such as 'Golden Boy'. When describing a bulb to nursery and garden store staff or a horticulturist, always use the scientific name to ensure accuracy. The encyclopedia and index in this book list many common names as well as the scientific names of every plant [see Encyclopedia of Bulbous Plants, pg. 95, and Index, pg. 134].

The world of bulbous plants also includes rhizomes, such as this windflower (left); tuberous roots, including the Persian buttercup (below); tropical bulbs, as for florist's amaryllis (bottom right); tubers, such as begonia (bottom left); and bulbous, perennial evergreens (not pictured).

SPRING BULBS

When we think of bulbs, the image most often in our mind's eye is of spring varieties. Spring-blooming bulbs include some of the most popular garden flowers: anemone, crocus, daffodil, hyacinth, iris, and tulip. Many other, rare or lesser-

known bulbs—including winter aconite, English and Spanish bluebell, cyclamen, fritillary, glory-of-the-snow, grape hyacinth, lily-of-the-valley, scilla, snowdrop, snowflake, and windflower—are also spring bloomers.

Consider that spring-blooming tulips are the world's most coveted bulbs; growers in the Netherlands produce more than nine billion tulip bulbs each year. Seven billion of these are destined for export to other countries, including the Netherland's number-one and number-eight markets, the United States and Canada. Billions more bulbs of other spring species are planted each autumn and early winter.

Spring bulbs are planted while they are at rest, then develop, sprout, and bloom when

The glory of spring bulbs stems from their vibrant color, which shoots through an awakening landscape still traced with snow or barren from winter. They refresh our spirit and remind us of the flowers that soon will be seen on landscape trees and in newly planted garden beds.

the weather warms. Some are early bloomers, blossoming when the ground first begins to thaw; others bear their flowers in mid- or late spring. After flowering is finished, the foliage lingers for a time, then turns yellow and withers as the bulb enters its dormant, or resting, phase.

In climates where conditions mimic those native to the bulb species, the bulbs can remain in the garden from season to season. If you live in such a climate, choose species tulips and daffodils that will naturalize—bloom each year and divide naturally —in your garden. They will bloom for many years, needing only occasional division as they become crowded and plants compete for nutrients [see Lifting and Dividing, pg. 76]. Gardeners in climates with conditions different from those natural for the bulb species should lift, cure, and store the bulbs to prevent decay, then plant them anew in the autumn as temperatures cool [see Curing and Storing Bulbs, pg. 81]. Some showy spring bulbs produce scant, diminutive blooms in their second and subsequent seasons; they should be dug and discarded after they bloom.

Spring bulbs paint color on gardens still filled with dwindling snow and winter-bare branches. You'll remember their beauty long after their petals drop and your beds are filled with blooms of annuals and perennials.

PLANTING DEPTH CHART

Inches
Surface
2
4
6
8
10
12
14

Tulip

Crocus

Persian Buttercup
(Ranunculus)

Windflower
(Anemone)

Hyacinth

Daffodil
(Narcissus)

Summer- and autumn-blooming bulbs blend eye-catching color and striking plant forms to create beautiful mid- and late-season beds and borders. Among the most popular summer bulbs are arum, tuberous begonia, caladium, calla, canna, dahlia, gladiolus, lily, ornamental onion, wood sorrel, and tuberose. For huge foliage and small yellow flowers similar to calla, try planting elephant's-ear. Add tender tropicals such as amaryllis, crocosmia, nerine, and veltheimia for the warmest months and hardy blooms for autumn—hardy begonia, colchicum, autumn crocus, cyclamen, lords-and-ladies, naked-lady, and rain lily—to fill a landscape with waves of riotous color until frost brings down the curtain.

SUMMER AND AUTUMN BULBS

Summer and autumn bulbs are available in garden centers and nurseries for planting in spring. They develop and bloom after moisture and rising temperatures trigger their growth. In mild-winter climates, some hardy varieties are perennial, increasing their numbers and their floral display as the seasons pass. In cold-winter climates, many summer and autumn bulbs require lifting and storage before replanting in the spring [see Curing and Storing Bulbs, pg. 81].

(Above) Pathways with seating areas and edges along fences are ideal locations to plant the tall summer bulbs such as gladiolus.

(Left) Autumn crocus gives a lasting salute to autumn long after the late-summer heat has exhausted most other flowers in landscape beds and borders.

Bunching rhizomatous bulbs—hardy begonia, society garlic, ginger, and ornamental onion, to name a few—tend to form dense colonies of new plants along their outside perimeter with the older plants in the center. Because competition starves the central plants of nutrients and moisture, they have fewer blooms of smaller size. Their colonies should be divided when they become too crowded [see Lifting and Dividing, pg. 76].

Lilies, including Asiatic, Oriental, and trumpet hybrids, along with dahlias are among the largest summer-flowering plants, creating distinctive floral displays that are central features for any landscape garden, border, or bed.

Freesia

Lily

Gladiolus

Bearded Iris

Florist's Amaryllis
(Hippeastrum)

Dahlia

Tuberous
Begonia

Cm
Surface
5
10
15
20
25
30
35

PLANNING CONTAINER GARDENS

You'll create colorful containers of bulbs by planting multiple species in a single pot, crowding in more plants than is usually done for in-ground use, and layering shallow-planted bulb species with those that are more deeply buried [see Planting Containers with Layers of Bulbs, pg. 49]. Follow these helpful ideas as you plan your container plantings of spring, summer, and autumn bulbs:

The best spring bulbs for containers are anemone, crocus, daffodil, hyacinth, and tulip. You can force early blooms by chilling the bulbs before you plant them [see Preparing Bulbs for Forcing, pg. 87]. Bulbs that have been forced, if kept, should be transplanted into the garden after they have finished blooming, although it may take several years for them to regain strength and bloom again. Other forced bulbs should be discarded.

Extend the brilliant color of bulbs through summer and into autumn. Good choices for summer bulb plantings in containers include tuberous begonia, caladium, dwarf dahlia varieties, and lily. For blooms later in the year, plant autumn crocus, cyclamen, and meadow saffron.

Regardless of the season, either massed plants of a single bulb species in a single color or a mix of several species of varied height make for striking container plantings. Very tall bulb varieties require lattice, stake, or wire supports, while midsized species create multiple levels in a large, deep container. For best appearance, flowers and foliage should stand at least one-third to one-half the container's vertical height above its rim. To keep the flowers coming along, use early and late varieties of the same or different species, layering the bulbs so that the late-flowering species— say, tulips—are beneath the early ones— such as grape hyacinth.

Plan to plant spring-blooming bulbs in autumn. Place the containers in a dark, cool, dry location where they will be protected from freezing temperatures, watering them weekly and allowing them to completely drain.

Summer-blooming bulbs can be planted as soon as the weather remains above 50°F (10°C) at night, usually mid to late spring.

Place the container in a location with filtered sunlight for 2–4 weeks before moving it into a spot that gets full sun. This method allows the bulbs to root fully before their foliage shoots and flower stems appear from the soil and begin to grow.

(Above) Grouped container plantings of bulbs are the right choice for both indoor gardens and small-space outdoor landscapes. They can fill a corner or accent a balcony or deck.

(Right) Choose a deep container with both ample drainage and sufficient room for roots to grow, and provide a loose soil mixture for your bulbs.

ARRANGING BULB CONTAINERS

Smaller containers look best when arranged in groups. Creating mixed floral displays of bulbs is easiest when containers with the same general appearance are planted with either a single species or layered multiple species that bloom in succession. Choose tall containers for deeply planted bulbs and shallow ones for smaller varieties. First, plant your bulbs [see Planting Bulbs in Containers, pg. 48]. When they begin to sprout, follow these steps:

Arrangements in Corners

1 Evaluate your site, marking its boundaries with masking tape. Mark a circle, rectangle, or triangle to define the outer perimeter of the display.

2 Line your tallest plants in front of green foliage or along a wall, or arrange them in an L-shape at a corner.

3 Divide midheight plants into two groups, one at each side and slightly in front of the row or L of tall plants.

Arrangements in Open Areas
If the group stands in an open area, place the tallest plants at the arrangement's center in a triangle or diamond shape.

4 Fill the space between and around the other containers with short plants.

BUILDING A WINDOW BOX BULB PLANTER

Window boxes add to the garden in two ways. They provide color high above landscape shrubs to adorn your home, while also framing your outdoor view with flowers. Window box planters are easy to build and install. This box features insert containers, allowing you to plant progressions of different bulbs. Grow each to blooming stage, then set them in the window box to provide constant, changing blooms. Gather the necessary materials, then follow these easy building steps:

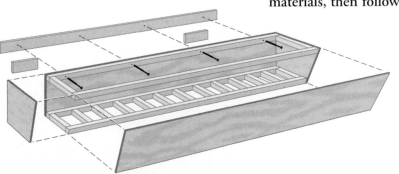

Required Materials:

From 2×2 (38×38-mm) dimensioned lumber:

2	59 1/16-in. (150-cm)	back rails
2	59 1/16-in. (150-cm)	front rails (see step #1)
2	9 1/2-in. (24.1-cm)	top crossbars
13	7 1/4-in. (18.4-cm)	bottom crossbars

From 15/32-in. (12-mm) ACX plywood:

1	10×60-in. (25.4×152.4-cm)	front panel
1	9 5/8×59 1/16 (24.4×150-cm)	back panel
2	10 15/32×9 5/8-in.×12 15/16×10-in. (26.6×24.4×32.9×25.4-cm)	end panels (see step #2)

Other components:

1	48-in. (122-cm) 1×4-in. (19×89-mm)	ledger
30	No. 8×3-in. (No. 8×75-mm)	deck screws
50	4d×1 3/4-in. (4d×45-mm)	galvanized finish nails
4	No. 8×1 3/4-in. (No. 8×20-mm)	lag screws
1	Qt. (1 l) exterior latex primer and paint	

1 Cut components. Cut frame and ledger pieces. Rip or plane a diagonal bevel on one face of each of the two front rails, 3/8 in. (10 mm) deep. Cut the front and back panels using a circular saw mounted with a plywood blade and scoring each cut with a utility knife to avoid face splits.

2 Cut end panels. Score and cut plywood to 9 5/8×23 15/32 in. (24.4×59.6 cm). Mark points on its top and bottom edges, 10 15/32 in. (25.4 cm) from the two opposite diagonal corners, joining the two points with a line. Mark, score, and cut the line to make two end panels.

3 Build bottom frame. On a layout table, set front and back rails parallel, with the front rail bevel facing outside. Mark points from the centerpoint of each rail, 4 in. (10 cm) on center from the centerpoint of each rail. Clamp, mark, drill 1/16-in. (1.5-mm) holes, and fasten each bottom crossbar into place with a deck screw.

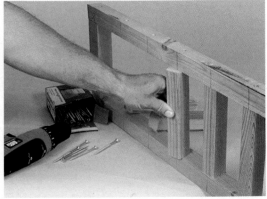

4 Build the top frame. On a layout table, set front and back rails parallel, with the front rail bevel facing outside. Flush a top crossbar with each rail end and clamp. Mark and drill 1/16-in. (1.5-mm) holes, then fasten with deck screws.

5 Attach back panel to the frame. Stand top and bottom frames on their front rails. Square and clamp the back panel flush with each rail end. Fasten the panel with finish nails spaced 4 in. (10 cm) on center.

6 Attach side panels. Square and clamp each side panel so it is flush with the beveled rail ends and with the back panel. Fasten with finish nails spaced 4 in. (10 cm) on center.

7 Attach the front panel. Square and clamp front panel so it is flush with the beveled rail ends. Fasten with finish nails spaced 4 in. (10 cm) on center.

8 Attach ledger. Use an electronic stud finder to mark the position of each casing stud under the window frame. Prime and paint the ledger. Position the ledger under the window sill, drill, and fasten it to the studs with four deck screws.

9 Install window box. Mark four points along the box's top back rail, 1 ft. (30 cm) on center. Drill 1/16-in. (1.5-mm) holes through the panel and rail. Add a decorative trim if desired, prime, and paint. Level and fasten the box to the ledger with deck screws.

PLANNING LANDSCAPES FEATURING BULBS

Bulbs are suitable for nearly every landscape. Whether in formal plantings—one based on repeated geometric patterns and symmetry—or natural, informal drifts, bulbs are a colorful focal point [see Designing Geometric Plantings in Small Beds and Borders, next pg., and Naturalizing Bulbs, pg. 36].

In fact, the first decision you should make as you begin to plan your garden is which of these approaches you wish to take. A good starting point is to visit public gardens and parks during the times of the year you want to feature bulb blooms. Many include extensive bulb plantings as part of their seasonal color offerings. Note the means used to define beds and borders, how they have mimicked the feel of natural woodlands, and how they have used small-space areas within the garden. Notice also the arrangements of bulbs within the planting areas, including their layout, color patterns, and textures.

At home, use a sketch pad and colored pencils to compare different planting arrangements in your own garden or landscape. Start with the arrangement of the beds themselves. Will you define their borders with edging materials, raise them to create new elevations and planes, or allow them to blend seamlessly into their surroundings? Will you plant several bulb species or match colors to create the effect you want? Will you have all the bed bloom together in one glorious explosion of color to celebrate the season, or should you plant a spectrum of early, late, and summer bulbs to create a long succession of flowers?

Consider how planting areas will look before and after the blooms have faded. Will you lift spring bulbs and replant with annuals, or will ground covers and perennials fill the bed? Should you plant early flowers, such as Icelandic poppy or viola, to fill in until summer bulbs bloom? Making these choices before you begin to select bulbs will save time and effort later.

Digital cameras are a great aid to note-taking when you wish to accurately remember the color, habit, flower form, or design elements of plants and plantings that you have seen during visits to garden shows, parks, arboretums, and private homes.

DESIGN IN COLOR

An artist's color wheel, found at art and hobby stores, is a useful tool for mixing and matching colors in your garden. The wheel has the three primary colors—red, blue, and yellow—interspersed with their complements—violet, green, and orange—in pie-shaped wedges around its outside edge. Some wheels include secondary hues interspersed between the primary and complementary colors.

To use the wheel, choose the color of one bulb you'll use. Its complement color will be found opposite it on the wheel's other side. For example, if you choose yellow tulips, you should complement them with blue violet, or with a range selected from the wheel between red violet and blue violet.

To create bright beds in full sunlight, mix pure primary colors; for a more subdued look that will suit dappled shade, choose pastel shades of the complementary colors. Both color schemes are attractive in the right garden setting.

DESIGNING GEOMETRIC PLANTINGS IN SMALL BEDS AND BORDERS

A small flower bed is a good choice for a formal bulb planting. Geometric plantings work well in square, rectangular, or round beds, because it is easy to divide those shapes as you arrange the plants and blooms. Here, you'll see how to plan a blue, red, and yellow bed to make a dramatic statement. If you prefer a subdued look to a contrasting one, simply substitute pastels. Gather a list of plants to include, and follow these steps:

1 If your bed is rectangular, draw an inset oval or circle touching its sides. For a circular bed, draw an inset rectangle. The inset divides the bed, creating four corner plantings for dark-colored, short-stature bulbs. Here, blue grape hyacinth will be planted.

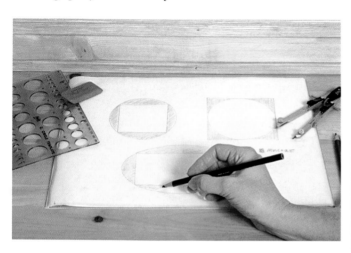

2 Next, divide the inner bed into quarters with a vertical and a horizontal line, or two diagonal lines, then inset its center with a bed one-third the size of the main bed, but with its same shape and proportions.

3 Plan to fill the center area of the flower bed with brightly colored, tall bulbs. In the example shown here, blue hyacinth bulbs will be planted.

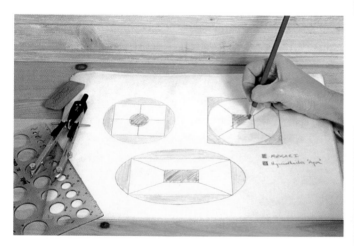

4 Between the center bed and the outer four, plant opposing beds each with midtone, midsized bulbs in opposing colors. Here, yellow and red hyacinth complete the design.

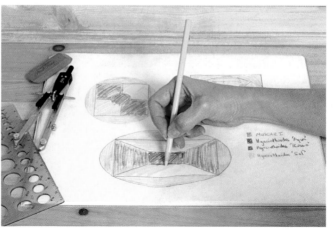

NATURALIZING BULBS

Woodland gardens and naturalized bulbs—random plantings of ground-hardy bulbs that increase naturally—are a good fit, whether beneath a grove of deciduous birch, aspen, or poplar, or erupting from a turfgrass lawn as a spring surprise. Choose one of the many options that are available for your garden.

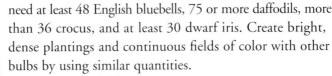

Spring-blooming bulbs in a dappled-shade location will create a wonderful landscape of bright, cheerful color punctuated by the grays and browns of tree trunks still awaiting the sprout of leaves. Garden color can appear before the last snows melt; plant crocus, glory-of-the-snow, snowdrops, and snowflakes, plus early-blooming *Iris reticulata* to cast winter's pall behind you.

Massed color is the secret to naturalized bulbs, so think in large numbers when planning a naturalized setting. For a small bed, you'll need at least 48 English bluebells, 75 or more daffodils, more than 36 crocus, and at least 30 dwarf iris. Create bright, dense plantings and continuous fields of color with other bulbs by using similar quantities.

Do as the British do when planting. Select the area carefully, marking drifts—sinuous, curved lines—along the curves of natural slopes, hills, and valleys, then scatter brightly colored markers—table-tennis balls work well—randomly into the area, planting a bulb where each falls. After you have completed a drift of one species, repeat the process with other bulbs until the site is crisscrossed with plantings.

For accents, plant irregular-shaped groups of smaller bulbs with the occasional tall one. A big patch of ground-hugging white and purple crocus at the base of a large landscape tree, punctuated with two or three clumps of tall yellow narcissus flowering at the same time, contrasts height and color attractively. Repeat several similar groups within the landscape for the best effect.

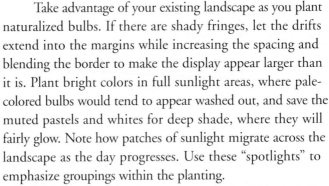

Take advantage of your existing landscape as you plant naturalized bulbs. If there are shady fringes, let the drifts extend into the margins while increasing the spacing and blending the border to make the display appear larger than it is. Plant bright colors in full sunlight areas, where pale-colored bulbs would tend to appear washed out, and save the muted pastels and whites for deep shade, where they will fairly glow. Note how patches of sunlight migrate across the landscape as the day progresses. Use these "spotlights" to emphasize groupings within the planting.

For summer bulb plantings, choose species that will bloom before or after perennial plants, shrubs, and trees in the garden. Flowering cherry, evergreen pear, and azalea, for example, will finish their bloom just as Spanish bluebell, lily, and reticulated iris begin their month-long displays. Dahlia, foxtail lily, lily-of-the-Nile, and pennants are among the garden's tallest bulbs; situate them where they will provide a glorious focal point for passersby to see.

DESIGNING NATURAL GARDENS FEATURING BULBS

Irregularly shaped beds are best for natural gardens. Naturalized bulbs are those species that reproduce and bloom with minimal attention. Species tulips, daffodils, and many other bulbs naturalize if their growing conditions—cyclical drought and moisture—are right. Mimic nature by copying its patterns as you plant, then allow your bulbs to multiply over a period of years. Choose varieties suited to your region, and follow these steps to plan your garden:

1 Measure your site and use tape or string to draw a circle in one of its corners, touching two of its sides. Divide this circle into quarters.

2 In an adjacent corner, draw another circle extending to the midpoint of the larger circle, again touching two of the bed's sides. Finally, in either opposite corner, draw an oval as long as the large circle and as wide as the smaller.

3 Rotate the bed within the site, if necessary, to fit the planting to natural contours, structures, and existing landscape plants.

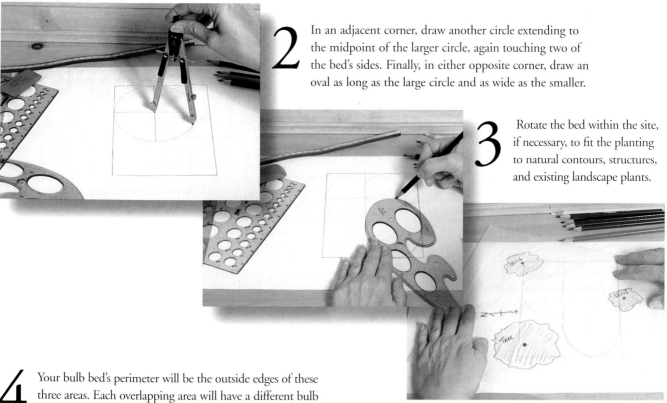

4 Your bulb bed's perimeter will be the outside edges of these three areas. Each overlapping area will have a different bulb variety planted within it.

5 When planning plantings within each area, mimic the curves of another area and plant them with different bulbs. Repetition of forms unifies the bed's composition.

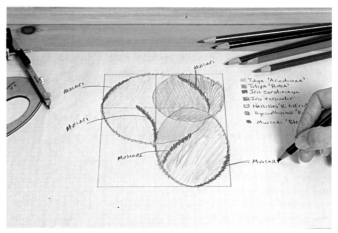

SITE IMPROVEMENTS

You've drawn your sketches and made your plans. Now take a few moments to consider adding structures and systems to enhance your garden's or landscape's appearance, reduce its care, make for easier access, and remedy any safety hazard.

First, consider drainage. Are there areas where water stands after a rain? Installing drain and pipe collectors to direct runoff is worth doing before the area is planted. Ensure runoff water is routed away from structures, including those of any neighboring homes. Enlist the aid of an engineer if the site is on a steep slope, and obtain any necessary permits before beginning construction.

Once you've dealt with any drainage issues, take a look at your soil. If it's compacted, add sand, organic matter, compost, and gypsum to help loosen it [see Preparing and Amending Soil, pg. 41]. Bulbs do best in well-drained soil, rich in decomposed organic matter. Dense or slow-draining soil can cause fungal disease and decay.

In addition to fertile soil, bulbs need adequate moisture. If rainfall in your region is frequent during the growing season, so much the better. In areas prone to intermittent rains or drought, consider putting in an in-ground irrigation system before you plant. Many hardware, home center, and garden stores have experts on staff to help you plan and install an automatic watering system scaled to your needs.

If you plan to use your garden at night, think about adding a low-voltage lighting system to highlight your flower beds, trees, and shrubs. An extra benefit is increased safety and security; walkways and stairs are more visible after twilight. Like in-ground irrigation, lighting can be easily planned and installed by most homeowners.

Finally, define your beds with formal or natural edgings. Edgings of brick, cast concrete, and timbers create a finished look and help make care easier when it comes time to trim lawn edgings. In natural settings use boulders or cobbles to add texture and interest to the site.

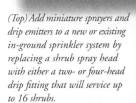

(Top) Add miniature sprayers and drip emitters to a new or existing in-ground sprinkler system by replacing a shrub spray head with either a two- or four-head drip fitting that will service up to 16 shrubs.

(Above) Install subsurface drain lines to remove standing water from low spots before you construct beds or begin to plant.

(Right) Enhance safety and extend your hours of garden enjoyment by adding a low-voltage lighting system to illuminate paths and steps, or to focus attention on your bulb plantings. Here, a walkway light spills onto a bed filled with colorful daylilies.

CREATING A PLANTING BED WITH BOULDERS

1 Mark the bed's outer edges with a hose. Cut turf inside with a sod-cutting tool, rolling it up in sections for removal. Reserve sod for site finishing after construction is complete.

Using local quarry or fieldstone boulders to define a flower bed's edges is an easy way to dress your bulb plantings. The planting area within the bed is filled with soil to raise it above the surrounding lawn, and the boulders provide a neat look. Many turfgrasses colonize new soil by sending out subsurface roots, or stolons, so plan to remove the turf where the stones will sit. Dig down at least 6 inches (15 cm) into the soil before bedding the boulders into sand. To build a stone-edged bed, follow these easy steps:

2 With a helper, examine each stone to choose its face side and move it to the outside of the bed's edge. Use a shovel to excavate a bed for each stone.

3 Add 2–4 in. (50–100 mm) of sand in the excavated bed, then seat the stone. Rock it to settle it into the sand, stopping when is becomes stable.

4 Continue placing the other stones, using a mix of low and high stones to define points of interest in the edge.

5 With the stones in place, fill the bed with topsoil. Tamp and water it to settle and fill all voids.

6 Fill any turfgrass voids using reserved sod removed from the bed's center. Dig planting holes according to your garden plan for your bulbs or bedding plants.

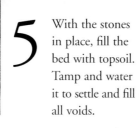

PREPARING SOIL FOR PLANTING

Bulbs can grow in nearly any soil, and you can help them produce great blooms by providing soil ideally suited to their needs. Three aspects of soil should be considered: porosity (how dense or loose it is), fertility (what nutrients it contains), and pH (its acid-alkaline balance). Most bulbs perform best in loose soil, balanced fertility, and conditions that range from slightly acidic to neutral. You can take these four steps to ensure optimum soil quality.

First, eliminate questions by testing samples of your soil or using a soil laboratory [see Soil Tests, this pg.]. Once the results are in, it's easy to improve your soil by adding recommended fertilizers or amendments.

SOIL TESTS

Soil test kits available in garden centers provide reliable results when used in accordance with their package instructions, measuring the three key nutrients—nitrogen, phosphorus, and potassium—and acid-alkaline balance. Alternatively, send your soil samples to a soil-testing laboratory; the USDA or Agriculture Canada extension office staff will provide recommendations.

Taking a proper soil sample is essential for achieving good results. Dig a hole 2 ft. (60 cm) wide and at least 1 ft. (30 cm) deep in the area to be planted. Using a clean hand trowel, scrape soil from the side of the hole, 6–8 in. (15–20 cm) from the surface. If the area is large, obtain several samples and mix them to create an average soil for testing. Seal the sample in a clean plastic storage sack until ready to test.

Follow closely and completely the test kit directions or the instructions provided by the soil-testing laboratory.

The results will include recommendations on amending and fertilizing.

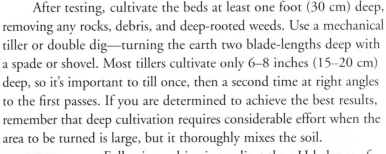

After testing, cultivate the beds at least one foot (30 cm) deep, removing any rocks, debris, and deep-rooted weeds. Use a mechanical tiller or double dig—turning the earth two blade-lengths deep with a spade or shovel. Most tillers cultivate only 6–8 inches (15–20 cm) deep, so it's important to till once, then a second time at right angles to the first passes. If you are determined to achieve the best results, remember that deep cultivation requires considerable effort when the area to be turned is large, but it thoroughly mixes the soil.

Following cultivation, adjust the pH balance of the soil. Most bulbs prefer slightly acidic soils, in the range of 6.0–6.5 pH, and few bulbs except iris can tolerate alkaline conditions. Lower pH by adding garden sulphur; raise pH by adding garden lime. Apply pH amendments following the package-recommended rates.

The next step is to apply fertilizer and amendments, working them into the loosened soil. Bulbs need three nutrients: nitrogen (N) for foliage growth, phosphorus (P) for vitality and strength, and potassium (K) for intercellular transport of nutrients. Their content in fertilizer is expressed numerically on the package. Use fertilizer with a 4–10–10 formulation when planting; you'll need extra nitrogen only if it's present in insufficient quantities. Bulbs also require micronutrients and trace minerals, including iron, magnesium, and zinc, best provided through amending and mulching with organic compost. Nitrogen is water-soluble and travels down through the soil, while phosphorus and potassium tend to become fixed where applied; for best results, mix fertilizers deeply into the soil.

Choices of fertilizers abound, including organic or inorganic, natural and synthetic, liquid or dry, foliar or water-soluble formulations. Note their nutrient contents rather than the names they are given.

While traditionally used for bulbs, avoid fertilizers containing bonemeal; several scientific studies suggest that bonemeal could be hazardous and may contain infectious proteins capable of causing fatal nerve disease in humans or in other animals. Bone meal also may lure animal pests by its scent.

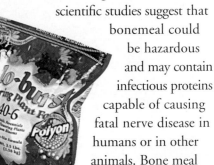

PREPARING AND AMENDING SOIL

Bulbs tolerate many different soil types and compositions. The best soils are loams—roughly equal mixtures of sand, silt, clay, and organic matter—with a slightly acidic pH. A soil test will tell you the amount and type of fertilizer to add, and whether an acid or alkaline amendment is needed. Regardless of additives, you will need to cultivate your soil to loosen it for planting, following these easy steps.

1 Begin first by turning over the soil in the bed with a shovel, breaking any clods and removing any rocks, roots, or debris. You should cultivate 12–16 in. (30–40 cm) deep.

2 Rake layers of organic compost and well-rotted manure to cover the bed, each 2–3 in. (50–75 mm) deep.

3 Work the compost and manure into the bed's soil with a shovel until it is evenly mixed.

Adding Compost to Sand or Clay

A Sandy soils drain too quickly and hold little moisture. Clay soils drain too slowly and hold too much water. Improve both soil conditions by adding a compost layer, 4 in. (10 cm) thick, and mixing thoroughly.

Correcting Soil pH

B Lower the pH of too-alkaline soil by adding garden sulfur, or raise it by adding garden lime as directed by your soil test. Ideal pH for most bulbs is 6.0–6.5.

C reating glorious bulb landscapes begins when, tools in hand and plans and ideas in mind, you plant your containers and landscape beds and borders. Choosing healthy, plump bulbs at your garden or home store, you'll prepare and plant floral displays that will add your personal touch to your home or garden.

You'll start at your garden retailer, in the pages of a direct merchant's catalog, or in the electronic marketplace, picking the best bulbs for your plant hardiness zone, climate, microclimate, and site. Once you obtain your bulbs, you'll head for your potting table or prepared garden beds to plant them.

Bulbs are ideal for small gardens and for decks, patios, or balconies, and they require suitable containers. In this chapter, you'll find tips for choosing the right planters and the steps to follow when preparing them for bulbs. You'll also learn how to create fabulous displays of blooms with plantings that feature a single bulb type in addition to those planted with several species in layers.

For landscape gardens filled with spring-, summer-, and autumn-blooming bulbs, you'll learn when and how to plant beds and borders, how to structure a mass planting for eye-catching color, how to plant in lawns and turfgrass, and how to create flowing, informal plantings with bulbs that appear as though fashioned by nature's own hand.

Various bulb types require special planting care. You'll be shown how to properly plant true bulbs, corms, rhizomes, tubers, and tuberous roots. You'll find instructions for the marking and planting of a formal bulb garden as well as approaches to follow for informal and casual beds.

You'll be encouraged to try planting beds and borders mixed with annual and perennial flowers to create season-long color in your landscape. Specialty gardens, including rock-garden beds featuring bulbs, are also shown with details on how to plant them.

Finally, you'll see the benefits of mulching over and around your bulb plantings, providing them with a blanket that protects them from unseasonably cold weather and naturally fertilizes and conditions your soil. Mulches prevent weeds from sprouting, reduce moisture loss, and keep your bulbs snug when frosts settle in.

The art and techniques used to choose healthy bulbs and plant them in pots, beds, and landscapes

Planting Bulbs

The lingering warmth of autumn's sun, mixed with the crisp night air and falling leaves, signals that it's time to plant spring bulbs. They'll use late-season warmth to break their dormancy, send down roots, and add moisture and nutrients to those already stored within.

CHOOSING BULBS

Like so much in life, your rewards for bulb planting depend on your contribution. As a first step to successful blooms, choose healthy bulbs, filled with vigor and ready to burst forth. How can you identify such bulbs in a garden store display? Look for these key features:

- **Size**—Bulbs that are large for the type have more volume to store nutrients and moisture than do smaller bulbs. They are better able to weather storage and handling. Some will produce multiple blooms.
- **Firmness**—Solid bulbs, heavy for their size, perform best. Such bulbs are generally free of fungal disease and excessive drying. Note that some tuberous roots and rhizomes naturally appear dry and withered.
- **Dormancy**—Bulbs that are dormant will be sprout-free, focusing early growth on establishing strong roots. If green sprouts are present, plant immediately.
- **Freshness**—Buy bulbs when they first appear in your garden retailer, storing them under ideal conditions if necessary until planting time arrives [see Bulb Planting Regions, pg. 25].

Garden retailers and nurseries usually stock spring-blooming bulbs in autumn and summer-, autumn-, and winter-blooming bulbs in spring, allowing you to plant them when the time is right for your area. Because stock may be limited, take advantage of direct merchants, including specialty bulb retailers that have unusual hybrids and cultivars rarely available in local, general gardening outlets. Pass by assortments, and choose the best individual bulbs available.

Wherever you obtain your bulbs, deal only with quality merchants whose staff are experienced in local growing conditions and your plant hardiness zone, avoiding close-out sales and out-of-season displays at retailers with limited garden knowledge.

(Top) When choosing bulbs, pick healthy ones, avoiding those with obvious signs of decay or mildew.

(Middle) The best bulbs feel heavy for their size because they hold ample supplies of water. Avoid bulbs that feel lightweight or already have become dehydrated and shriveled.

(Above) Select bulbs that are healthy and lack cuts, bruises, and gouges that could cause decay after planting.

(Right) Acquire your bulbs with a specific effect in mind. Know the size of your bed and the number of bulbs needed to fill the area before choosing cultivars for their color and habit. Allow an extra 10 percent for safety.

CHOOSING HEALTHY BULBS Healthy bulbs are easy to spot: they're large, heavy for their size, firm, and free of bruises, soft spots, mold, or cuts. Pick your bulbs when they're fresh, soon after they arrive in garden stores or appear in catalog listings. Spring bulbs are available in autumn, and summer and autumn bulbs in spring. To choose healthy bulbs, make your choice of varieties, then follow these steps:

1 Many garden retailers display their bulbs in convenient bins with photographs of the blooms and planting information about them. Use their pictures to help pick varieties that match your selected color combinations.

2 Carefully inspect each bulb, choosing large, solid bulbs. Avoid those with premature sprouts, cuts, and signs of mold or shriveling. Those that have superficial splits in their onionskin-like coverings are acceptable.

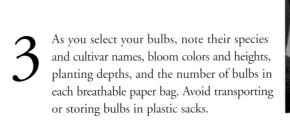

3 As you select your bulbs, note their species and cultivar names, bloom colors and heights, planting depths, and the number of bulbs in each breathable paper bag. Avoid transporting or storing bulbs in plastic sacks.

BULBS IN CONTAINERS

Atrip to a garden store or nursery will reveal the myriad choices of containers. You can select pots that fit your decor, and vary shapes and sizes for added visual interest. Be sure the containers you choose provide sufficient space for the species they'll hold, insulate the soil within from rapid temperature changes, and offer ample drainage while retaining adequate moisture.

As you consider containers for your outdoor floral bulb displays, keep these key points in mind for best results:

- **Size**—Bulbs need space for their roots to grow and for soil to support their stems. Always pick large, deep containers that are able to accommodate your bulbs at the proper planting depth, with room to spare.
- **Porosity**—Porous terra cotta allows plant roots to breath, while thin plastic walls may overheat in sunlight. Select containers made of insulating materials, paint clay pot interiors with breathable latex sealant, and place thin-walled containers inside insulating, decorative, ceramic pots.
- **Drainage**—Bulbs require good drainage to avoid fungal diseases. Choose containers with drain holes, or plan to drill them yourself. Use a layer of porous landscape fabric, pea gravel, or pottery shards to keep soil and roots from clogging the drains.

Containers drain rapidly, are susceptible to drought, quickly lose water-soluble nutrients, and may overheat in direct sun. You can counter these tendencies with careful placement, frequent watering, and regular feeding during active growth with either granular or foliar—leaf-absorbed—fertilizer until flower buds form.

Keep in mind that large pots filled with bulbs, soil, and water are heavy; always use care and lifting aids to move them. Set them on sturdy supports or stands able to hold their weight.

Once you've selected suitable bulbs and containers, look again at your display site to note its growing conditions: wind exposure, hours of sunlight, temperature, and access for care. Note that the sun will be lower in the sky during early spring than it appears in early autumn. Prepare a temporary storage area for planted spring containers that is dark, cool, and semi-dry, and remains at 35–40°F (2–4°C). The best locations are in sheltered but unheated garages and sheds, except for the very cold-winter climates, where unheated basements are ideal. Check the pots periodically and keep their soil barely damp.

Bring your container of bulbs out of storage and into its final display location after the flower buds have formed. Remember that its display of colorful blooms will last longer if the spot has cool conditions.

TRANSPLANTING SPROUTED BULBS

Garden retailers and florists frequently offer bulbs ready to bloom in nursery containers. Most have been forced—held in cold storage, then moved to sunny warmth and allowed to sprout and bloom [see Forcing Bulbs, pg. 88].

Plant such bulbs in your garden or in an indoor container while protecting their roots. Cut away the outer plastic pot, then transplant the bulbs, soil and all, to a new, larger container or hole in the soil of the planting bed. Match the soil level of the original container, and then water heavily to compact the surrounding soil.

Water transplanted bulbs until the soil is soaked during the first few days, then water only when the soil is dry to the touch.

Forced bulbs rarely bloom in their second season, but if cared for properly, they will regain strength and bloom in later years.

SELECTING AND PREPARING CONTAINERS

Picking the right bulb container starts with your choice of bulbs. Each species has a specific planting depth—a good rule of thumb is 3 times the bulb's height—and specific soil needs [see Encyclopedia of Bulbous Plants, pg. 95]. The container should be at least 3 inches (75 mm) deeper than the planting depth and have adequate drain holes. Choose and prepare your containers for planting by following these steps:

1 Choose containers that are made of insulating materials to keep your bulbs from overheating. Best are ceramic, insulated composite plastic, terra cotta, and wood.

2 Add more drain holes, enlarge any that are too small, or drill your own, using a power drill that is fitted with a ⅜-in. (9-mm) masonry bit.

3 If you reuse containers, sterilize them in a solution of 1 part household bleach and 9 parts water. Wear protective clothing and gloves. Dry pots overnight before planting.

Warning

Household bleach is made with sodium hypochlorite, a powerful skin and eye irritant. Avoid hazard by wearing gloves and protective clothing whenever you handle bleach solution.

4 Reduce deposited mineral salts on porous pots such as terra cotta by painting the interior of the pots with a breathable latex sealant. Dry the sealant overnight before planting, and soak the terra-cotta pots in water before use.

PLANTING BULBS IN CONTAINERS

Once your containers have been prepared by sterilizing them, drilling drain holes, sealing porous terra cotta, soaking porous materials, and installing pea gravel or pottery shards to protect their drain holes from blockage, it's time to plant your bulbs [see Selecting and Preparing Containers, previous pg.].

Single-species plantings, whether of spring, summer, or autumn bulbs, are somewhat easier than those of mixed multiple species. Avoid mixing spring and summer bulbs in the same container; their planting times, care needs, and growing conditions are very different.

To plant a single type of bulb, note its recommended planting depth, a measurement usually 3–4 times the bulb's height [see Encyclopedia of Bulbous Plants, pg. 95]. Partially fill the container with loose potting soil, compacting it until the distance from the soil's surface to a point 1 inch (25 mm) below the rim of the container is equal to the recommended planting depth. Next, arrange the bulbs in the container, spacing them closely together; container plantings are made closer than those recommended for outdoor gardens. Finally, cover the bulbs with soil and water them, and allow the container to drain before placing it in storage until sprouts emerge. A cool, dry location safe from freezing is appropriate for spring bulbs; a sheltered outdoor area with filtered sunlight is best for summer and autumn bulbs.

The most colorful pots of bulbs are packed with several species to create a layered effect of different plant heights. Layering extends to the technique used to plant the container, as the smaller, shallow-depth bulbs are planted above their larger, deeper-depth, companion species.

FERTILIZING CONTAINER PLANTS

Container plantings of bulbs quickly deplete potting soil of its nutrients. Water-soluble compounds such as nitrogen are depleted as they leach from the soil in the draining water after the pots are irrigated.

Keep bulbs healthy after their shoots emerge from the soil by applying liquid organic 10–5–5 fertilizer at one-half the package-recommended rate each time you water, usually weekly or semi-weekly.

Foliar fertilizers are another option. They are sprayed onto the growing plants and absorbed directly through the bulb's foliage, bypassing the soil and roots.

Discontinue fertilizing just before your bulbs flower. Water until the foliage begins to shrivel, then cease. When the foliage has turned brown, store the bulbs in their pot of dry soil in a dry, warm spot out of direct sunlight, or lift the bulbs to cure, clean, and store them.

Tropical bulbs should be fed regularly during periods of active growth.

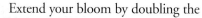

Extend your bloom by doubling the number of bulbs, staggering them vertically and alternating early- and late-blooming varieties of the same species. Plant the late-blooming variety beneath the early bloomer for best results.

You'll have even more colorful containers when you layer several different species of bulbs [see Planting Containers with Layers of Bulbs, next pg.]. Layering is the technique of stacking different bulb types that require varying planting depths vertically in the soil. If possible, plant deep, late-blooming species on the bottom, then shallower types above them. Tulips and crocus are one popular combination, but many other striking options are available to explore.

PLANTING CONTAINERS WITH LAYERS OF BULBS

Layer your containers to grow several different bulbs for simultaneous bloom, or plant species with different bloom times to extend the season. Three or four layers of bulbs are planted in turn, with bulbs requiring the greatest planting depth at the bottom and the smaller bulbs above them. Gather your bulbs, potting soil, and container, and follow these steps:

1 Line the container's bottom with pea gravel or porous landscape fabric to collect moisture below the soil and allow it to drain.

2 Fill the container with 3 in. (75 mm) of potting soil, then compact it with your hands. Next, add large, deeply planted bulbs, slightly crowding and evenly spacing them.

3 Orient the first bulbs so that their pointed end is facing up. Cover them with potting soil. Measure the depth and add or remove soil as necessary.

4 Add a second layer of bulbs, spacing them evenly. Cover them with soil, and repeat with other bulb types for third and fourth layers, as desired.

5 Fill the container with soil and level it to about 1 in. (25 mm) below the pot's rim. Water thoroughly to settle the soil and allow the container to drain.

PLANTING BULBS

Outdoor bulb plantings require unique planning and preparation. In the following pages, you'll learn about each of the most popular planting methods to use with many types of bulbs in almost every garden setting.

For the best results, it's important to properly position most true bulbs, corms, and rhizomes. Plant bulbs and corms with their platelike bases down, and pointed ends up. Roots will develop from the base, and shoots will extend from the growth point. Rhizomes usually are elongated and tubelike in form; place them horizontally in the planting hole at the recommended depth for the specific bulb. They will sprout from the latent buds. Tubers and tuberous roots have multiple growing points and will develop roots and shoots in the proper locations regardless of their orientation at planting time. If a bulb gives few clues to its orientation and the location of its basal plate, plant it on its side. Its roots and stems will develop properly, bending if necessary to reach the surface or extend downward.

To fertilize when planting, dig the planting hole, trench, or bed 4–6 inches (10–15 cm) deeper than you plan to place the bulbs, cultivating and adding 10–10–5 fertilizer or enriched compost to the soil below each bulb, then backfilling over it with unamended soil to the proper planting depth. Keeping fertilizer beneath the bulbs yet separate helps prevent fungal disease while ensuring that phosphorus and potassium will be available in their root zone. For large areas, it's best to amend the soil when it is prepared for planting [see Preparing Soil for Planting, pg. 40]. Better yet, fertilize and amend the soil a week or so before you plan to plant. This resting time permits cultivated soil to settle and fertilizer to dissolve.

Following a layout plan is the best way to ensure good results when you plant bulbs. Divide the bed into planting areas using string. Position the bulbs according to your plan, filling each area and spacing them as recommended.

PLANTING INDIVIDUAL BULBS, CORMS, RHIZOMES, AND TUBERS

Most bulbs are planted individually. It's the right approach for planting small areas, or for as many as 30 bulbs. Planting single bulbs is ideal when you want to create sinuous drifts in a naturalized garden or for making bulb accents in your borders. Gather a bulb planting tool, hand fork, your bulbs, and planting depth information for each species, then follow these easy steps:

1 Note the planting depth for the bulb species and check that each bulb is free of decay, mildew, or cuts. Discard any bulbs that have become dehydrated.

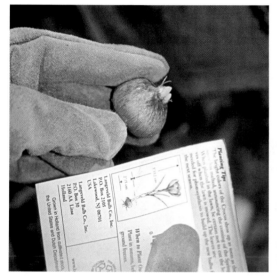

2 At the site, use a bulb planting tool to excavate a hole 2 in. (50 mm) deeper than the recommended depth. Add 10–10–5 fertilizer and cover it with 2 in. (50 mm) of soil.

3 Determine the top of the bulb. Turn it so its pointed end is up and its platelike base or the roots are down. For tubers, or if orientation is unclear, plant the bulb on its side. Place the bulb in its hole.

4 Check your final planting arrangement after all of the bulbs have been placed. Relocate bulbs to fill any sparse or skipped spots.

5 Fill the holes with soil. Gently press the soil over each bulb to ensure good soil contact and eliminate any air pockets. Water the planting thoroughly.

PLANTING
IN BEDS

Group plantings—many types of bulbs in a single plot—make for memorable beds and borders. Whether you're planning a formal, informal, or naturalized garden, mixed plantings are suitable.

Planting a formal bed or border requires time spent creating the patterns in which the bulbs will grow [see Planting Formal Beds, opposite pg.]. It's best to use string, hose, or rope to diagram the pattern at the site since they are easily rearranged and shifted. You can choose from many patterns for your bed: squares, rectangles, ovals, and circles. These, in turn, can be divided by halves or thirds, bisected by diagonals, or inset with grids and concentric patterns. Remember the keys to a formal bulb planting are straight lines, geometry, and symmetry, with matching colors repeating several times as recurring elements.

Naturalized beds are more free-flowing than their formal counterparts. Curves replace straight lines, and the bed's edges blend instead of meet. Sinuous forms, including kidney and paisley shapes, create drifts of color that appear as if spilled by Mother Nature upon the landscape. Though they're subtle, planned forms also are used in these informal gardens, and they incorporate many of the same rules as those for geometric plantings.

In a border, plan to step the plants' bloom heights down from back to front as you progress through the planting, so each succeeding tier of bulbs is taller and able to be seen over the ones in front of them. Beds are really back-to-back borders, with their tallest plants in the center and shorter species to the edges.

Bulbs seem made for planting into well-defined beds. Because these landscape features are separate from most structural elements and surrounding plantings, they easily can be planted with summer and autumn bulbs after the spring bulbs fade, giving a seasons-long display of color.

Use edging materials or plant double, staggered rows of bulbs to create frames for your patterns in a formal garden, and remember blocks of contrasting colors are attractive and eye-catching. For naturalized plantings, blend the color palette through a range—from red to red orange, for instance, or orange to yellow—to disguise and blend the forms.

PLANTING FORMAL BEDS

1 Use a shovel to excavate the bed until it is 2–3 in. (50–75 mm) deeper than the planting depth of the largest bulbs you will plant.

The same layering technique used for containers can be employed with in-ground beds [see Planting Containers with Layers of Bulbs, pg. 49]. When making formal bulb displays, excavating the planting hole and planting layers of bulbs is easier than digging individual holes for each bulb. Choose bulb varieties that bloom at the same time or season. Gather your shovel, measuring tape, planting depth information, fertilizer, stakes, string, and bulbs, and follow these easy steps:

2 If animal pests are attracted to the garden, line the bed with galvanized hardware cloth of ½-in. (12-mm) wire mesh.

3 Apply 10–10–5 granular fertilizer at the package-recommended rate. and then backfill over the fertilizer with 2–3 in. (50–75 mm) of soil.

4 With stakes and string or plastic garden tape, mark the pattern to be used in the bed.

5 Plant the first layer of bulbs. Space them evenly, changing colors between areas. Cover them with soil to the next layer's depth. Here, tulips form the first layer.

6 Plant the second layer of bulbs. Cover them with soil to the top layer's depth. Late-blooming yellow daffodils form the central accent in this bed.

7 Plant the top layer of bulbs. Here, mixed crocus and grape hyacinth form an outer border.

LANDSCAPE BULB PLANTINGS

When bulbs are used for color on a scale fitting for a large landscape, it's best to divide the area into sections, each with its own plantings. An area situated beneath paired trees, for instance, might be suitable to host an overlapping pair of circular plantings. A winding cleft between two natural rises could be mirrored in parallel drifts of bulbs that mimic the existing curve provided by your setting.

There is no single design for landscape plantings. You might relate adjacent areas by repeating elements in a different color or with another species of bulb. A large circular planting, for instance, might have two smaller, irregular satellites nearby enclosing single, circular flower plantings that are remniscent of the larger bed.

Another design technique is to create triangles between group plantings, then use their end points as boundaries for creating trenches filled with drifts of naturalized bulbs [see Planting Landscapes: Trench Plantings, next pg.]. Use two, fully overlapped obtuse triangles to fill an irregular, U-shaped planting area, with central primary colors blending in shades to complement the edges. There are as many variations as there are landscapes.

Choose one site as a focal point for the bloom; you might consider having that focal point move as the garden season progresses. Plant the first highlight with early spring bulbs such as crocus and glory-of-the-snow, a second with late spring bloomers such as lily-of-the-valley and flag iris, a third with midsummer lily and gladiolus, and a final one with autumn crocus and meadow saffron. Over the seasons, your landscape will boast ever-changing color patterns.

LAYERING

Layering is a planting technique as suitable for landscapes as it is for containers, and it works similarly in both cases.

Pick bulbs of different species with different depths of planting. Choose either bulbs that will bloom at the same time or those that will bloom in succession.

Prepare the soil, then dig planting holes, trenches, or excavated areas as deep as the deepest species you will plant. Backfill, then plant again with a shallower, smaller bulb. Repeat as many times as desired for a layered, mixed-bulb planting of great beauty.

As you plan your plantings, remember to allow access to every area of the yard by planning bulb-free paths across any bed wider or deeper than 4 feet (1.2 m). This will provide a comfortable reach from either side for weeding or cultivating. You can disguise the paths by making them sinuous or by following a planting's edge.

Planting in large areas—plus lifting and storing numerous bulbs later—requires considerable time and effort. Develop your landscape in stages by implementing elements of your overall plan one feature or garden area at a time over a period spanning weeks or months.

(Top) Grape hyacinth is a good choice for edgings and for solid blue areas in formal garden plantings.

(Above) Snowflakes of different species bloom in spring, summer, and autumn with delicate grace.

(Below) Hardy begonia mixed with white and blue lily-of-the-Nile make a patriotic edging.

PLANTING LANDSCAPES

Landscape plantings usually call for bulbs to be set in trenches or large areas rather than individually planting them. A trench or the entire bed is excavated, bulbs are placed, and then the trench or area is filled. Gather a shovel, bulb fertilizer, planting depth information, your bulbs, and a hose, and follow these steps:

Trench Plantings

1 Dig a trench that is 3–4 in. (75–100 mm) deeper than the desired planting depth.

2 Apply 10–10–5 formulation granular fertilizer at the rate recommended on the package. Backfill over the fertilizer with a soil layer 3–4 in. (75–100 mm) deep.

3 Orient and place each bulb at the recommended spacing. Press them firmly into the soil.

4 Cover the bulbs with soil and thoroughly water the planting to help settle the soil.

Area Plantings

1 Excavate the bed 3–4 in. (75–100 mm) deeper than the desired planting depth, while carefully avoiding the major roots of nearby trees.

2 Apply 10–10–5 granular fertilizer at the package-recommended rate. Rake it into the soil.

3 Backfill with soil over the fertilizer using a layer that is at least 3 in. (75 mm) deep.

4 Orient and place the bulbs at the recommended spacing. Press each firmly into the soil. Cover with soil. Water thoroughly.

NATURALIZED PLANTINGS

You probably have seen a naturalized planting of spring-time bulbs, stunning in its simplicity and alive with color. Such plantings are generously large, attractively mix several species of bulbs, or gloriously highlight a single species, and seem to have erupted spontaneously from the soil at the gardener's beckon.

At its most basic, naturalizing means planting bulbs informally. We throw markers over our shoulders with our eyes closed in search of an ideal, random broadcast that mimics nature's patterns.

Naturalize bulbs that are hardy in your climate to avoid having to lift and store scores of bulbs hidden in your landscape. Many beautiful cultivars lose vigor in a season or two; match them with crocus, narcissus, and species tulips that are hardy in your zone [see USDA Plant Hardiness Around the World, pg. 132]. It's a good idea to choose bunching bulbs—bluebells, grape hyacinth, and snowflake, for instance.

If you live in a cold-winter climate, naturalize early-blooming spring bulbs in your lawn [see Naturalizing in Turf, next pg.]. By the time the grass requires mowing, glory-of-the-snow, snowdrop, and squill will be entering dormancy.

Match your naturalized bulbs and site with conditions needed for them to thrive. Shelter drought-loving summer bulbs beneath overhangs and deciduous trees in areas prone to summer rain. Choose quick-draining slopes and hills, especially those with open exposures and facing the sun.

(Right) Decorative grass plantings and areas of lawn are good spots for naturalized spring bulbs.

(Below) Multilevel rock gardens planted with naturalized bulbs have a charm that becomes more colorful with each passing season.

NATURALIZING IN TURF

Spring bulbs are delightful when they poke out of a turfgrass lawn, meadow, or woodland. Most grasses grow slowly or are dormant until the weather warms in spring, seldom needing mowing. Plant naturalizing bulbs beneath the turf and allow them to flower amid the grass. Gather stakes and string, a turf cutting tool, tarp, fertilizer, planting depth information, your bulbs, and a bulb-planting tool, and follow these steps:

1 Mark your accent areas or the drifts to be planted using stakes and string or plastic garden tape.

2 Use either a turf-cutting tool or a sharp spade to remove blocks of sod with roots, 4–6 in. (10–15 cm) deep. Set aside on a tarp.

3 Orient and place your bulbs, using your site design plan. Use a bulb-planting tool to dig each hole 3 in. (75 mm) deeper than the recommended depth.

4 Apply 10–10–5 fertilizer at the package-recommended rate. Backfill the hole with soil, 3 in. (75 mm) deep.

5 Set the bulbs into the planting hole and cover them with soil. Tamp the soil with your palms.

6 Replace the sod. Tamp each turf block to ensure good soil contact. Water thoroughly.

MIXING BULBS WITH ANNUALS AND PERENNIALS

Mixing bulbs in your landscape with other flowering plants—annuals and perennials—provides you the best of both flower worlds. Mixed beds make your landscape colorful all season long. They begin with a bloom of spring bulbs, segue to colorful seeded annual plantings or bedding plants, then make way for the simultaneous blooms of summer bulbs and flowering perennials, and wrap up with a final show of autumn-blooming bulbs as nights turn frosty.

Provide growing conditions that will keep both your bulb and flower plantings healthy. Bulbs need periods of drought to force them into dormancy and avoid fungal disease, while annuals and perennials require consistent irrigation [see Watering Bulbs, pg. 66]. Divide your beds with clearly defined watering zones so you can apply or withhold water as needed. Drip irrigation systems that deliver pinpoint watering are an ideal solution; set one circuit of your automatic irrigation controller to water the bulbs according to their needs, a second for the annuals, and a third for perennial flowers, shrubs, and trees.

Deep-rooted, drought-tolerant annuals and perennials are the best companions to most bulbs. Globe amaranth, baby's-breath, Dahlberg daisy, common geranium, lavender, and morning glory are the best choices to mix with hardy begonia, dahlia, society garlic, lily, and ornamental onion. For full-sun locations in early spring, mix Iceland poppy with daffodil and tulip for contrast in color and foliage. In shade, surround bluestar, Canterbury-bells, and forget-me-not with plantings of anemone, bluebell, and bleeding heart.

Clearly mark bulbs that require lifting; ice cream sticks make good, shallow markers. Place the markers as the bulb foliage begins to yellow to signify the locations for digging after the leaves have withered.

(Above) Showy florist's amaryllis and annual impatiens bedding plants are good companions in a sunny or filtered-sun spot.

(Right) Bearded iris mix with oriental poppy and evergreen shrub plantings. The effect they achieve is well-suited to this free-flowing, natural landscape.

PLANTING A MIXED ROCK GARDEN

1 Use stakes, string, or plastic tape to mark the places where trees and shrubs will be planted, then define the bulb and flower planting areas.

Rock gardens are a natural fit for many bulb, shrub, and flower plantings. The stones define the bed and draw your eye, framing the plants. Place your landscape stones and install any permanent bed residents first, beginning with trees and woody shrubs. Then plant naturalizing bulbs and perennial flowers, finishing with annual bedding plants or seeds. Gather stakes, string, a shovel, bulb-planting tool, fertilizer, bulbs, plants, and seeds, and follow these easy steps:

2 Install your trees and shrubs in planting holes as deep as and twice the width of their original nursery containers or rootballs. Mark each planting hole for later reference.

3 Use a shovel to excavate bulb planting areas, fertilize, plant, and cover. Mark the spaces you will plant with inset summer bulbs and perennial flowers.

4 Place your perennials into their reserved sites. Avoid disturbing newly planted trees, shrubs, and bulbs.

5 Rake the soil around the plantings. In spring, plant summer and autumn bulbs, and seed annual flowers (or plant them as bedding plants). Apply mulch to retain moisture and block sunlight from weeds.

PLANTING SUMMER AND AUTUMN BULBS

Warm weather's arrival signals planting time for summer- and autumn-blooming bulbs. In general, you should wait until the soil has warmed thoroughly, an event that lags behind the arrival of warm days if cool evenings persist. To be certain, wait until the air temperature remains consistently above 60°F (16°C) for at least 10 days before planting summer and autumn bulbs.

Lily, though, is unique. Lilies are hardy and should be planted as soon as the soil can be worked. Lily bulbs also are susceptible to drying out when stored, so acquire them early in the season and plant them immediately. If you must store them for a time until unseasonably cool, wet weather moderates, do so in slightly moist peat moss held in a dark area at about 40°F (4°C) [see Curing and Storing Bulbs, pg. 81].

The remaining, tender bulbs—tuberous begonia, caladium, calla lily, canna, dahlia, and gladiolus—sometimes sprout early growth before planting conditions are right. If this happens, go ahead and plant them, protecting them with a bed cover when frost is likely. Pound stakes into the ground across your planting area, spacing them at regular intervals. Then spread and anchor clear plastic fabric, punching airholes every 12 inches (30 cm) or so to permit the soil to breathe. The stakes will support the plastic above the shoots, preventing direct contact with the foliage. In milder climates, apply an insulating mulch.

Taller species such as some dahlia, gladiolus, and lily require stake supports when exposed to wind. Ties should allow some stem movement to bolster sturdy growth and help the plants resist breakage.

Remember to thoroughly water new summer bulb plantings in order to restore moisture, compact the soil around the bulbs, and trigger the end of dormancy. Apply mulch to the planting area to provide a neat appearance, retain moisture, insulate the soil, and block weed germination [see Mulch and Bulbs, pg. 62].

Three popular summer bulbs are dahlia (top), gladiolus (middle), and lily (bottom).

(Right) Planting summer bulbs such as begonia and dahlia is easiest when you have all of your tools and supplies close at hand. You'll need a bulb-planting tool, trowel, hand fork, pruning shears, and watering can, as well as a bag of starter fertilizer.

PLANTING ROOT DIVISIONS

Plants with rhizomatous and tuberous roots differ from true bulbs by sprouting from growth points, or crowns. With careful division and planting, these crowns will increase the number of plants in your garden [see Dividing Tubers and Rhizomes, pg. 80]. Most such plants are first acquired in nursery containers rather than as dormant bare roots. To plant rhizomes and tuberous roots, follow these steps:

1 Consult plant-care tags for specific planting information. Planting depths vary by species, from partial burial to depths of 6 in. (15 cm).

2 Dig a planting hole 2–3 in. (50–75 mm) deeper than the depth of the soil in the nursery container and half again as wide. Add 10–10–5 fertilizer as the package directs. Cover the fertilizer with soil, 2–3 in. (50–75 mm) deep.

3 Carefully invert the nursery container, supporting the rootball and stem with your hands. Tap the container, allowing the plant to slide into your open hand.

4 Untangle any encircling roots and place the rootball into the planting hole. The soil's surface should match that of the rootball.

5 Fill around the plant with soil. With your open palms, gently press the soil around the rootball. Water each division thoroughly after planting.

MULCH AND BULBS

Many bulbs, including those that are shallowly planted, seem to tolerate soil temperature fluctuations, though outright freezing and thawing cycles may dislodge them from the soil and break their roots. But it's still a good idea to protect your plantings with mulch that helps regulate the surface soil temperature, retains moisture, and hinders the germination of weed seeds. Mulch has a neat appearance and helps keep the cultivated soil's surface open so that it absorbs water without runoff.

When selecting mulch, opt for organics rather than rock, plastic, or sand. Mulches made of plant matter decompose slowly, improving the soil texture and releasing nutrients. As organic mulches break down, soil bacteria first absorb nitrogen and oxygen, robbing shallow-rooted weeds of nutrition without affecting the deeply rooted bulbs. Later, they release the mulch's nutrients and fertilize your beds.

Soil is a good insulator—temperatures at shallow depths frequently remain constant unless cold air is accompanied by chilling rain, and because many bulbs are planted deeply, they are protected from sudden frosts. Mulch adds even more insulation, further reducing temperature fluctuation. Shredded bark and leaves, wood chips, organic compost, ground cocoa and rice hulls, and weed-free straw are good choices. Avoid the use of sphagnum and peat as a mulch for your bulbs, though; water tends to run off them without being absorbed, and the rare natural bogs in which they form are threatened by depletion and overharvest.

Apply mulch in a layer, 1–2 inches (25–50 mm) thick. Sprouting bulbs will push through the mulch as they grow. For summer bulbs such as gladiolus and lily, rake the mulch away from their stems once their foliage has emerged to avoid creating too-moist conditions and harboring fungal spores that could promote disease on their stems. A clear circle 2 inches (50 mm) in diameter usually is sufficient.

Where bulbs will overwinter in your garden, apply mulch heavily in autumn to extend its insulating benefits and naturally fertilize your soil. Mulch also helps to protect the soil from freeze-thaw cycles that sometimes can uproot bulbs.

After you plant (top), apply mulch to help insulate the soil, prevent freeze-thaw cycles, and hold soil moisture. Here, dry pine needles have been chosen because they both protect the bulbs and add nutrients and acid to the soil as they slowly decay (middle). By spring, the needles will emerge from the melting snow (above).

(Right) The bulbs that were planted and mulched with pine needles will sprout, grow buds, and burst into flower.

MULCHING AROUND BULBS

Mulch performs many useful tasks for your bulbs and dresses your landscape. Use organic mulches—wood chips, fine ground bark, compost, salt hay, or cocoa hulls—for best results. Apply mulch before bulb sprouts appear. Use a garden cart to carry the mulch, together with a mulching rake, to the site, then follow these steps:

1 Begin by dumping cartloads of mulch at several points within the flower bed. The contents of a full 5-cu. ft. (0.15-m³) cart or barrow will cover a 15–20-sq. ft. (1.4–1.9-m²) area.

2 Use a mulching rake with long tines to spread the mulch over the bed surface in an even layer, 3–4 in. (75–100 mm) deep.

3 If your bed includes trees, shrubs, or perennial plants and you live in a humid climate, keep mulch 4–6 in. (10–15 cm) from their trunks or stems.

C are of your bulbous plants, you'll be pleased to know, is easier by far than for most other landscape plants. Established bulbs are strong, resistant to drought and limited nutrition, and are susceptible to fewer pests than other plants.

The care they require is limited to regular watering when needed, occasional fertilizing, and inspection to prevent disease or a pest infestation from becoming established. In this chapter, you'll learn how much water to apply and when to irrigate, how to apply fertilizer at the correct rate, and what to look for when it comes to pests and disease.

You'll see how good garden practices and care techniques limit the spread of harmful insects, bugs, and nematodes, and how to use these beneficial organisms as your controls. For each pest, disease, or care condition, you'll find a recommendation for an environmentally positive way to treat your bulbs.

Animal pests—mice, gophers, moles, and larger mammals such as deer, raccoons, opossums, and household pets—are a challenge to any garden. Many bulbs are popular as food for these pests, but you'll find that they can be discouraged by barriers installed at your garden's perimeter, under the ground, or around the bulb planting itself.

Caring for Bulbs

Later in the chapter, you'll be given specific care instructions for lifting, dividing, curing, and storing each of your favorite bulbs so you can enjoy blooms from them each and every season. This information includes the right temperatures, humidities, and storage cycles for many types of bulbs, as well as suggestions for curing them prior to storage, helping them to adjust to dormancy, and preparing them for growth in succeeding years.

You'll also find tips on dividing rhizomes and tuberous roots when they begin to compete with one another, and be shown how to propagate bulbs—grow new plants from your offsets, cuttings, bulblets, and bulbils. You will also be invited to try your hand at growing a new hybrid bulb from seed—one way to have a truly personal and unique bulb garden.

Finally, you'll be introduced to some advanced propagation techniques that growers use to multiply plants.

Learn how to water, feed, and protect bulbs, plus tips on storing them and propagating new plants

---

The Persian bellflower, commonly known as ranunculus, should be watered regularly from the time it is planted until its blooms fade. For the best displays, fertilize the planting from the time shoots first emerge in spring until the bulbs form flower buds.

WATERING BULBS

(Right) Dahlias come in all sizes, from the diminutive to the very tall. The largest cultivars have dish-sized blossoms.

(Below) Most bulbs store water within for use when supplies become spotty. You should water your bulbs during their period of active growth whenever natural precipitation becomes sparse.

Provided you've selected bulbs suited to your plant hardiness zone and climate, they will require remarkably little care. Of their few needs, regular in-season watering is most important.

Remember that most bulbs developed traits in the wild suited to the specific climate in which they grew. They survived periods of drought by entering a near-dormant state, and will do the same in your garden. Water may come from rain or from irrigation; your role as gardener is simply to ensure that they receive a regular supply of water during the times that they break dormancy, grow, bloom, and store nutrients for the coming dormant cycle.

Generally, keep spring-blooming bulbs moist with regular waterings from the onset of warm weather until their foliage matures; water should be withheld thereafter, either by natural drought or by lifting and storing them in a warm, dry location after their foliage has dried [see Lifting and Dividing, pg. 76].

Summer and autumn bulbs require watering throughout the entire gardening season, from spring planting until temperatures cool. Reduce the amount of water to summer bulbs as autumn arrives, triggering their dormancy. Continue to water your autumn bloomers until the first frosts begin in cold-winter climates, or until the onset of winter in mild-winter areas. Move them indoors into cool, dry storage until spring [see Curing and Storing Bulbs, pg. 81].

For evergreen and tropical bulbs, withhold water to slow their growth, generally starting about 6 weeks after their blooms fade, then begin watering again to prompt another bloom cycle, provided sunlight hours remain long. Some tropicals require other watering schedules; follow the recommendation for the species.

The question is how often to water and how much to apply? A good rule is to wait until the soil dries, then slowly apply 1 inch (25 mm) of water—envision an imaginary sheet of water that thick—covering the garden soil until it is saturated 4–6 inches (10–15 cm) deep.

SEASONAL WATER NEEDS BY BULB BLOOM TIME

Water your bulbs using the recommendations found here. Note whether the bulb is a spring-, summer-, or autumn-blooming type, then find the specific bulb and match it to its care needs. Water regularly for the period shown, then either withhold water or lift, cure, clean, and store the bulbs at the beginning of the resting period. Always store lifted bulbs in conditions that will help avoid fungal disease or excess drying [see Curing and Storing Bulbs, pg. 81].

For other bulbs, follow the general care instructions or refer to the grower's instructions contained on the bulb's package.

Spring-blooming Bulbs:
Florist's cyclamen, glory-of-the-snow, Persian butter-cup, snowdrop, snowflake, star-of-Bethlehem (spring), spring starflower, windflower: *keep moist autumn–spring.*
Baboon flower (spring), cape cowslip, corn lily, freesia, squill: *keep moist autumn–summer.*
Crocus, daffodil, hyacinth, tulip, wood hyacinth: *keep moist winter–spring.*
Dog-tooth violet, fritillary, fumaria, grape hyacinth, striped squill, woodlily: *keep moist in spring.*
Blood lily, bugle lily, camas, Dutchman's-breeches,

fan iris, Mariposa lily, lords-and-ladies, wood sorrel: *keep moist spring–summer.*
Jack-in-the-pulpit, kangaroo-paw: *keep moist spring–autumn.*
Calla lily, lily-of-the-valley, southern swamp lily, star grass, wake-robin, winter aconite: *keep moist year-round.*

Summer-blooming Bulbs:
Hardy begonia, tuberous begonia (summer), caladium, canna, lily-of-the-Nile (deciduous), false lobster-claw, montebretia, pineapple lily,

IRRIGATING BULBS

Regular watering during active growth—usually performed weekly—is essential to making your bulbs grow and bloom. If the soil around bulbs becomes dry, they slow their growth and prepare for dormancy; extended drought will halt their bloom. Note the amount of water received from rains during the time that the bulbs are sprouting new foliage and sending up buds, and apply more if needed. For most species, the soil should remain evenly damp or moist. If a dry spell lasts more than a week, gather your hose and a diffusing nozzle in the morning after the air has warmed, and follow these steps:

1 Overhead watering is best for most bulbs. To gauge the amount to apply, place clear plastic cups in several places in the planting you'll water.

2 Apply water evenly. If the water begins to run off, allow a few minutes to pass, then reapply water until the soil is saturated.

3 When your test cups have filled with an inch of water, the bed should be watered adequately.

4 Carefully dig down about 6 in. (15 cm) with a hand trowel, avoiding any bulb stems, to see if the water has penetrated at least that far into the soil.

Scarborough lily, society garlic, tree gloxinia, tuberose: *keep moist spring–autumn.*
Blazing star, daylily, elephant's-ear, fire lily, gladiolus, bearded iris, gloriosa lily, torch lily, lily-of-the-Incas, bush morning-glory, bitter Indian nasturtium, orchid pansy, spider lily, tiger flower: *keep moist spring–summer.*
Habranthus, summer hyacinth: *keep moist spring.*
True lily: *keep moist spring–summer.*
Dahlia: *keep moist summer–first frost.*
Blackberry lily: *keep moist midsummer–early spring.*
Aztec lily: *keep moist summer–early spring.*

True amaryllis: *keep moist midsummer–early spring.*
Freesia, snowflake (summer), star-of-Bethlehem (summer), wandflower: *keep moist autumn–spring.*
Baboon flower (summer): *keep moist autumn–summer.*
Ornamental onion: *keep moist winter–spring.*
Ginger, true gloxinia, flag iris, zephyr lily (summer): *keep moist year-round.*

Autumn-blooming Bulbs:
Peacock orchid: *keep moist spring–summer.*
Meadow saffron, naked lily, nerine, snowflake (autumn), winter daffodil: *keep moist autumn–spring.*

Tropical and Evergreen Bulbs:
Florist's amaryllis, false lobster-claw, society garlic: *keep moist spring–autumn.*
Elephant's-ear, peacock orchid: *keep moist spring–summer.*
Habranthus: *keep moist until late spring.*
Florist's gloxinia, lily-of-the-Nile (evergreen), Scarborough lily, star grass, zephyr lily (semi-evergreen): *keep moist during active growth; reduce watering for 1–2 months after bloom has been completed to rest the plant.*

FERTILIZING BULBS

Fertilizer applied when the beds were prepared for planting will have provided all the necessary nutrients to get your bulbs off to a good start [see Preparing Soil for Planting, pg. 40]. Now regular applications of nitrogen, phosphorus, and potassium, plus micronutrients and trace minerals, are essential for root and foliage development, bloom development, and flowering.

Always read and completely follow all the package directions when applying fertilizers, wear protective clothing, and safely dispose of all empty containers and unused fertilizer solutions as directed. Water thoroughly both before and after the fertilizer has been applied to dilute, dissolves and spread the nutrients that it contains.

Feed spring bulbs with a 10–5–5 dry or granular fertilizer, work an enriched organic compost into their mulch, or spray their foliage or flower shoots with a foliar fertilizer that will be absorbed directly. Apply fertilizer once a month until the bulbs' buds begin to open.

Fertilize summer, autumn, and evergreen bulbs monthly during periods of active growth, using a balanced 10–10–10 dry formulation, liquid organic fertilizer, or foliar plant food. Withhold fertilizer from the bulbs once they have formed flower buds.

Always work granular fertilizer into the soil with a hand fork or a garden rake to mix it with the soil. If you have applied mulch, rake it aside, apply the fertilizer, then work it in. Water thoroughly immediately after you apply the fertilizer to carry its nutrients down into the soil and dilute it, preventing foliage burn.

PREDORMANCY FERTILIZING

In most cases, it's a myth that spring bulbs require predormancy fertilizing; the one exception is in beds with naturalized bulbs.

For most bulbs, it is more important to leave the bulbs' foliage in place after all their bloom has finished. Their leaves will manufacture nutrients and store them underground in the bulb, new corm, or tuber, allowing it to grow and bloom the following season. After a month or so, the foliage will yellow and wither away. Trim away spent seed pods and flowers after bloom, leaving the foliage to do its work.

Avoid predormancy feeding; instead, it's best to apply a fresh layer of protective mulch to the bed. It will decompose slowly, releasing its nutrients into the soil and be available for the bulbs' use when they begin to grow new roots and foliage.

For naturalized beds that contain bulbs which remain in place from year to year, withhold water beginning in autumn. In spring, or when shoots or flower stalks first emerge from the soil, apply a 0–10–10 formulated liquid fertilizer and immediately water to carry it deeply into the soil. Phosphorus and potassium quickly bind chemically to soil mineral particles, remaining fixed at the surface. Watering helps carry them to the bulbs' root zone. If the bed can be cultivated and the location of the bulbs is certain, cultivate carefully around the plantings to mix the fertilizer into the soil.

Annually, give your soil a boost, especially container plantings. Decomposed kelp extract contains few nutrients but holds many enzymes that foster root development and activate growth points on bulbs. Apply it annually in springtime.

HOW TO FERTILIZE

Bulbs that are lifted after they bloom require fertilizing only when active growth begins; use lifting as an opportunity to cultivate your soil and work in amendments for the following season [see Preparing and Amending Soil, pg. 41]. Naturalizing bulbs should receive annual fertilizing as they begin their growth cycle. Gather the appropriate fertilizer, a shovel, a rake or hand fork, and gloves, and follow these steps:

Fertilizing New Plantings

1 Use 10–10–5 granular fertilizer or fertilizer formulated as bulb food. Apply to the bottom of planting holes or areas dug 3–4 in. (75–100 mm) deeper than the bulb planting depth.

2 Use a hand fork or rake to thoroughly mix the fertilizer into the soil as you loosen it.

3 Fill over the fertilizer layer with 3–4 in. (75–100 mm) of native soil to avoid fertilizer contact with the bulb, then plant your bulbs.

Seasonal Fertilizing

1 When the ground thaws in spring, before shoots appear, carefully rake away any mulch from around the bulbs. Wait for bulb sprouts to emerge.

2 Use 10–5–5 granular fertilizer for spring bulbs and 10–10–10 for summer bulbs. Spread fertilizer around the base of the plants. Avoid contact with their foliage.

3 With a hand fork or rake, mix the fertilizer into the soil surface. Thoroughly water to dissolve nutrients and carry them into the soil.

4 Apply new mulch around the plants to conserve water and help control sprouting weeds.

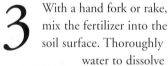

PESTS AND DISEASES

Bulbs are surprisingly resistant to pests and disease than are many other flowering plants, but you should remain vigilant. Begin your control of pests and disease with good gardening practices designed to reduce the chance of infestations or infections. Block the growth of weeds that host insect pests and fungal spores by mulching your beds or planting ground covers; promptly remove any weeds that emerge. Rid your garden of fallen leaves, plant debris, pruning litter, and dead foliage to eliminate the favorite hiding spots of slugs and snails, two of the most significant bulb pests. Garden debris shelters eggs, larvae, grubs, and adult insect pests, as well as nematodes and many plant bacteria, viruses, and fungal spores.

One way to dispose of garden waste and put it to good use is by composting it. The heat of vegetative decomposition renders most pests and weed seeds inert, leaving you with rich organic compost suitable for your garden. Organic compost contains beneficial living organisms, and it provides major and trace nutrients to feed your plants. It also is a great soil conditioner for improving soils that are too clayey or sandy.

Next, take advantage of the disease and pest resistance of some bulb species. Daffodil and other narcissuses, for example, have natural defenses against fungus, insect, and animal attack. Good cultural practices by growers mean that bulbs are vigorously checked while in product fields so they are in good health and free from pests and disease when they arrive at the garden center, nursery, or your home. Using care to avoid cuts and nicks during planting and cultivating further helps to keep fungal disease spores from entering the bulb.

Still, sometimes pests gain a foothold. Ants, aphids, Japanese beetles, various borers, mites, mollusks (slugs and snails), harmful nematodes, thrips, whiteflies, and wireworms feed on bulbous plants. Some bulbs are susceptible to botrytis, mildew, and viral diseases.

Friend or foe? About 95 percent of the insects found in your garden are either beneficial or harmless. Many bulb plants are resistant naturally to many insect pests, which you can control with simple means such as washing them off with a sharp stream of water. Ladybird beetles—ladybugs— eat several times their weight in aphids each day and are available at garden centers.

Most horticulturists refer to the USDA's guidelines for Integrated Pest Managment (IPM) to keep infections and infestations to a minimum. IPM calls for frequent inspections to discover outbreaks before they become widespread, followed by the use of hand controls—picking, crushing, washing with plain water, and the like—to eliminate the condition. Persistent conditions first are treated with biological measures—releasing ladybird beetles to eat aphids, applying beneficial nematodes to the soil, or spot spraying solutions containing *Bacillus thuringensis* (BT)—then by using mild, environmentally protective controls such as household and insecticidal soaps that smother or dissolve pest tissues. These sequential steps will control most insects and diseases.

Only the most severe, sustained outbreaks should be treated with pest-specific pesticides and fungicides. If such care is necessary, choose a control that lists both the pest or disease condition and is intended for use on your specific plant. Always read and completely follow all package directions for mixing, diluting, timing, frequency, and method of applying the control. Wear protective clothing and a respirator, apply the agent as directions state—avoiding broadcast application—and dispose properly of unused solution and empty containers.

The goal of IPM is to limit damage to the garden while protecting the environment and maintaining a healthy ecological balance between insect pests and predators. Pests reproduce more rapidly than do predators, so maintaining a healthy population of predators assures that pest insects and bugs are kept to a minimum.

BULB PEST AND DISEASE SOLUTIONS

Symptom	Cause	Remedies
Curled, twisted, sticky leaves; stunted or deformed blooms; loss of vigor. Sometimes found within tunic covering of lifted bulbs.	Aphids. Look for clusters of 1/16-in. (1.6-mm) black, green, yellow, or gray round insects. Frequently found in association with ants that milk them for their honeydew secretions.	Release ladybird beetles, lacewings. Spray with water from a hose; spray with solution of 2–3 T (30–44 ml) dishwashing liquid per gallon (4 l) of water; spray with insecticidal soap.
Spotted, sometimes semi-translucent leaves, frequently accompanied by fungal disease.	Stem borers. Look on foliage, roots for segmented larvae and caterpillars, 1/2–1 in. (12–25 mm) long. In corn-farming regions, corn borer may infest dahlia, gladiolus.	Hand pick; apply *Bacillus thuringensis* (BT) to affected foliage. Remove and destroy infested foliage.
Stunted plants; white cottony clusters in leaf axils.	Mealybugs. Look in the junctions between leaves and stems or at the base of leaf clusters for white or gray, waxy bugs, 1/8 in. (3 mm) long.	Dab or spray with rubbing alcohol diluted 3:1; spray with insecticidal soap; spray with horticultural oil.
Stunted, discolored, spotted plants with deformed roots, sometimes bearing swollen galls; loss of vigor.	Nematodes. Microscopic wormlike creatures that live in soil and feed on plant roots.	Release beneficial nematodes. Remove and destroy affected plants. Replant with unrelated species. Solarize bed for 3–4 weeks prior to planting by covering soil with clear plastic and allowing sunlight to raise soil temperature to 140°F (60°C).
Leaves speckle, wrinkle, turn yellow, drop; minute white webs are seen on undersides and at basal junctions.	Spider mites. Shake foliage and blossoms over white paper and look for moving red or yellow, spiderlike specks. Thrive in hot, dry conditions.	Release ladybird beetles. Spray repeatedly with water to rinse off dustlike pests; spray with insecticidal soap. Avoid use of sprays that kill natural predators.
Brown-, silver-, or white-speckled leaves; may be gummy or deformed. Blooms are deformed and fail to open.	Thrips. Shake foliage and blossoms over white paper and look for moving, winged specks. Thrive in hot, dry conditions.	Release ladybird beetles. Spray with water; spray with insecticidal soap; avoid use of sprays that kill natural predators. Remove and destroy infested foliage.
Chewed leaves and blossoms; silvery mucus trails.	Slugs and snails. Look after dark for shelled and unshelled mollusks on foliage or soil.	Remove leaf litter, which is used as a hiding place. Hand-pick after dark; use copper foil barriers around beds or containers; dust with diatomaceous earth; use non-toxic baits containing iron phosphate; use bait gel.
Uprooted plants; foliage eaten to ground level; bulbs and roots eaten, leaving dying foliage stalks and leaves.	Deer and rodents. Look for hoof and paw prints, burrows, mounds, tunnels.	Plant resistant bulb types. Install fence barriers or cages when planting, including beneath-soil barriers. Trap and remove. Avoid bonemeal use.
Browning flowers and foliage collapse under heavy fuzz of gray or brown fungal spores.	Botrytis. Also known as gray mold, a fungal disease. Common in warm, humid weather.	Remove affected blossoms, foliage, or entire plant; space plants for more air circulation; reduce nitrogen fertilizer; remove mulch; water early in day to allow complete drying before nightfall.
Powdery black or brown dusting on foliage and blossoms; leaves may drop.	Leafspot. A fungal disease. Common in shady, massed plantings.	Remove shading foliage, increase air circulation; spray with sulfur fungicide.
Light powdery dusting of gray or white on leaves, flowers; deformed new growth; stunting; loss of vigor.	Powdery mildew. A fungal disease. Common if humid, warm days and cool nights alternate.	Remove shading foliage, increase air circulation; spray affected plants with solution of 1 T (15 ml) baking soda and 3 T (44 ml) horticultural oil to 1 gallon (4 l) water; dust with sulfur.
Streaked and mottled foliage; deformed blooms; stunting; loss of vigor.	Mosaic virus. An incurable plant disease.	Remove and destroy affected plants. Promptly control aphid, spider mite, thrip infestations, which can spread viral infection. Plant resistant bulb types.

TREATING FUNGAL DISEASE

Most bulbs are naturally disease-resistant. Viral diseases, such as mosaic, resist treatment; if your bulbs contract a virus, lift and discard them to prevent spreading. Most bulb diseases are caused by fungus or mold, and they are more common in cool, damp weather. Prevent them by watering early in the day and allowing foliage to dry thoroughly before sunset. If your bulbs experience an outbreak of disease, you'll need a fungicide that lists on its label both the specific condition to be treated along with your plant, a plastic spray applicator, eye protection, rubber gloves, and water-proof clothing, as needed. For best results, follow carefully and completely these instructions:

1 Identify the disease to be treated. If necessary, consult experienced staff at your garden store or nursery. Choose a control that is approved for use on your bulb plants.

2 Wear protective clothing and gloves. Read completely and follow exactly the package instructions for mixing and applying the fungicide.

3 During a wind-free period, fill your spray applicator with correctly diluted solution. Spray only the affected plants, wetting the tops and undersides of all foliage. Avoid overspraying.

Warning

Garden fungicides, herbicides, and pesticides pose personal hazard if ingested or upon contact with skin or eyes. Always wear eye protection, gloves, and protective garments when you mix, pour, apply, or dispose of any garden chemicals.

4 Empty the sprayer and wash it and your gloves with warm, soapy water. Always safely dispose of unused solution, wash water, and empty garden chemical containers.

APPLYING INSECTICIDAL SOAP

1 Identify the pest to be treated. If necessary, consult experienced staff at your garden store or nursery. Choose a soap solution that is approved for use on your bulb plants.

Soaps, when used alone or in combination with plant-derived pesticides such as pyrethrin, kill pests by interfering with their breathing or by dissolving their cell walls. To be effective, they must be applied directly to the pest. Use them only when an infestation continues after using hand control, biological controls, and washing with plain water. You'll need an insecticidal soap that lists on its label both the specific condition to be treated along with your plant, a plastic spray applicator, eye protection, rubber gloves, and waterproof clothing. To choose a control and apply insecticidal soap, follow these instructions:

3 On a morning free of wind, fill your spray applicator with soap solution. Spray pests, wetting both the tops and undersides of all infested foliage. Avoid overspraying or application to uninfested plants.

2 Wear protective clothing and gloves. Read completely and follow exactly the package instructions for applying the insecticidal soap.

Warning

Insecticidal soaps can contain pesticides that pose personal hazard if ingested or upon contact with skin or eyes. Always wear eye protection, gloves, and protective garments when you mix, pour, apply, or dispose of any garden chemicals.

4 Empty the sprayer and wash it and your gloves with warm, soapy water. Always safely dispose of unused solution, wash water, and empty garden chemical containers.

ANIMAL PESTS

Once mammals develop a taste for bulbs, ridding your garden of them can require persistence, effort, and ingenuity. Most damage is due to eating, uprooting, and trampling. Common bulb pests in gardens include birds, deer, gophers, mice, moles, opossums, raccoons, voles, and woodchucks— even household cats and dogs.

Avoid enticing these animal pests to your garden by choosing to skip applications of strong-scented fertilizers, including fish emulsion and bonemeal [see Preparing Soil for Planting, pg. 40, and Fertilizing Bulbs, pg. 68]. Instead, use unscented organic fertilizers such as composted or other well-rotted manure, organic compost, or natural mineral phosphate.

Another deterrent is to plant bulbs that mammals and birds find distasteful: daffodil, hyacinth, narcissus, and ornamental onion among the spring bulbs, and anemone, begonia, calla lily, canna, dahlia, and meadow saffron of the summer bulbs.

Open-topped cages for planting bulbs are available at garden stores and nurseries. Install them as you would a wire cage. Plant your bulbs within, safe from most burrowing animals.

To keep animal pests out of gardens, create barriers above and below the ground around their perimeters, remembering that to be effective they must block both tunneling and jumping. Mature deer regularly leap fences as tall as 8 feet (2.5 m), though two lower fences spaced about 4 feet (1.3 m) apart, especially if electrified, seem to deter them. Gophers, moles, voles, and woodchucks dig burrows and tunnels as deep as 2 feet (60 cm); bury wire mesh fabric of ½-inch (12-mm) gauge at least that deep as a barrier to secure your garden.

The best barrier defense from animals is to build and bury wire mesh cages in your beds, planting the bulbs within the cages [see Protecting Bulbs from Rodents, next pg.]. Your bulbs will grow through the cage's wire cells, remaining protected until they divide beyond the boundaries of the cage.

Many products are offered that claim to make gardens distasteful to animal pests. They include decoys, noisemakers, devices that vibrate, others that move in the wind, and topical ointments made of urine from wolves and dogs. Some of these appear to work for a time, but all lose effectiveness as pests become accustomed to them.

Animal pests that can dig up or otherwise damage your bulb plantings include opossum (top), mice and other rodents (bottom), as well as household pets. Limit the damage from all three sources by using only unscented organic fertilizers, avoiding bonemeal, fish emulsion, and fish meal.

PROTECTING BULBS FROM RODENTS

Burrowing animals such as gophers, squirrels, moles, mice, and opossums destroy bulbs by eating or dislodging them. Protect your plantings by building a simple cage of wire cloth fabric and planting your bulbs inside. Measure the area of the bed to be protected; you'll need a bit more than twice as much wire cloth of ½-in. (12-mm) gauge. Also gather a pair of wire cutters, a straight-edged board, measuring tape, a shovel, and your bulbs, and follow these easy steps to build and install your cage:

1 Unfold a cardboard box and use it as a pattern. Make three parallel cuts into each side of the wire cloth fabric, 8 in. (20 cm) deep, to create four flaps. Use the straight-edged board to crease the wire.

2 Fold the flaps in and the sides up to form a cage. Crease and fold the top of the cage to form a lid. Dig a hole in the bed to install the box.

3 Fertilize and fill the bottom of the box with 2–3 in. (50–75 mm) of soil. Orient and space your bulbs in the soil.

4 Fill the box with soil, close the lid, and wire it to the sides. Then cover the box with soil. The bulbs will sprout through the mesh that protects them.

LIFTING AND DIVIDING

Lifting is the careful digging of bulbs after their flower displays have faded, they've stored nutrients for the next growth cycle, and all their foliage has died. Lifting bulbs is necessary for those with gardens in areas where climate conditions—such as cold, heat, humidity, and precipitation—would cause their bulbs to experience dampness when dormant, be subjected to freezing, or suffer dehydration or damage due to overly high soil temperatures. By comparison, dividing rhizomes or separating bulbs renews and propagates new plants when the originals become too crowded.

(Right) It's best to use a garden fork to lift bulbs, lifting them before their stems and leaves have dried and detached. Beginning your dig a short distance away from the bulbs, plunge the fork vertically into the soil, then lever the handle down to lift the soil and bulbs. Separate the bulbs from the soil as you go, moving across the bed.

(Bottom) Bulbs such as daffodil and tulip naturally produce new bulbs—offsets—that can be detached, cured, stored, and planted the following season.

Bulbs can remain in the soil from season to season in those areas that mimic their natural growing conditions. Mediterranean climates—such as those found along the Pacific Coast—are hospitable to many of the spring bulbs that originated in southern Europe and the Middle East. Southern California, the Gulf states, Florida, Hawaii, and other mild-winter, semi-tropical climates support in-ground cultivation of evergreen varieties and summer bulbs that would be lifted in cold-winter climates.

Lift spring bulbs after dormancy's onset to retain their health and vitality. As foliage yellows, mark its position to aid location after it withers and is removed during garden care. Dig carefully from the outside margins of the bed with a garden fork, loosening the soil from deep below the bulbs and revealing them. Shake them to remove any clinging soil, then lay them on a tarp or newspaper to dry in a warm, dry spot sheltered from the sun [see Curing and Storing Bulbs, pg. 81].

Most bulbs will have produced offsets, bulblets, bulbils, new tubers, or root divisions. New plants from small bulblets and bulbils require several seasons before you will obtain blooms [see Harvesting and Planting Offsets, pg. 79]. Discard the small bulbils and bulblets unless you plan to grow them in nursery rows. Carefully clean and separate larger offsets and tubers from the parent bulbs; they can be planted the following season and may bloom then or in the following year.

Plants with rhizomatous and tuberous roots form dense, clumping colonies that periodically require division, usually several years after planting. Bulbs in the center of these colonies lack sufficient water and nutrients; they tend to be stunted, have diminished blooms, or fail to bloom entirely. To renew their vigor and obtain new plants for other areas of your garden, they should be divided after lifting [see Dividing Tubers and Rhizomes, pg. 80].

Some bulbs lack onionskin-like tunics and can be subject to dehydration unless they are protected and given moisture after lifting. Store them in breathable containers packed in slightly moist peat moss.

LIFTING BULBS

1 When foliage first begins to yellow, mark the location of the bulbs to lift so that they can be found easily a few weeks later.

Bulbs need a period of semi-dormancy and rest after their foliage withers. In regions with frequent summer rains, or in others with cold-winter climates, bulbs should be lifted and stored after they have completed their growth cycle for the year. It is also a good idea to lift any bulbs that have grown crowded, dividing them and holding them for later planting. You'll need a garden fork, a fabric tarp or piece of burlap, and a warm sunny day. Follow these steps:

2 Begin at the bed's edge, at least 1 ft. (30 cm) from the nearest bulbs. Use a garden fork to plunge vertically into the ground and lift up the soil. Set it aside. Work your way toward the bulbs.

4 Gently brush any clinging soil from the bulbs. Place them in a shady spot to dry, spaced in a single layer on a tarp or burlap sack cloth.

3 As you near the bulbs, angle the fork, inserting it under the bulbs and lifting up to free them. Take care to avoid cutting through the bulbs.

PROPAGATING BULBS

Already, varied supply of fresh, healthy bulbs is available each year from garden and direct retailers. Many gardeners prefer to plant new bulbs each year; some cultivars and climates demand that you do so. For those who prefer to grow new plants from their own bulbs—propagate them—it's relatively easy to harvest offsets, and divide rhizomes and tubers to create fresh plants.

Propagation also includes techniques that require greater patience and skill. Some lily plants, for instance, grow bulbils in the leaf axils—the point where the leaf joins the stem. Bulbils can be cultured to grow new individual plants. It's also possible to create new plants of tuberous begonia and dahlia by taking stem cuttings of fresh shoots, rooting them, and allowing them to form bulbs. [see Advanced Techniques, pg. 82].

Still another method frequently used is to grow new hybrid bulbs from seed. If a flower stalk remains on the bulb after its bloom fades, it will swell and form seed. Offspring grown from the seed are not the same as their parent, but a cross-hybrid of the original plant with pollen from another. Their growth habit, bloom color, and form may differ greatly from either of the parent plants.

Divide your bulb plantings when they become crowded. The lily-of-the-Nile in this front yard started as single plants. In the span of just a few years' time, they have formed crowded groups and the time has come to divide them if they are to remain attractive.

Harvesting and culturing bulb seed is somewhat more challenging than for other garden seeds, but with experience it is easily mastered. Try your hand at harvesting and culturing bulb seed by allowing the seedpods to fully develop and turn brown and brittle. Crack them open over a sheet of clean, white paper to release their tiny seeds.

COMMERCIAL BULB PROPAGATION

Growers carefully develop new bulb varieties, called "hybrid cultivars", by dusting pollen from the anther of one parent plant onto the stigma of another. The results are entirely new bulbs.

Many thousands of new combinations are created each season, most destined for obscurity. A few of the hybrids, plus even fewer chance mutations called "sports," are cultured and distributed to garden stores and nurseries.

Those plants that exhibit unusual blooms, striking color, disease and pest resistance, or cold hardiness are ideal for reproduction and propagation.

Growers use plant tissue culture or other advanced techniques to clone exact duplicates of their most promising bulbs. Even with such advanced techniques, a dozen years may pass before they are available for marketing to gardeners.

Label and store the seeds in individually sealed containers in the vegetable keeper of your refrigerator for 2 months. Then plant them in loose, rich, moist, sterile potting soil and raise them under glass at 62–75°F (16–24°C). Uncover when they sprout, watering whenever the soil starts to dry. Then transplant them outdoors in spring, lift, and over-winter them indoors until they mature.

HARVESTING AND PLANTING OFFSETS

1 Carefully separate large offsets from the parent bulb, using a sharp knife if necessary to avoid damaging the bulbs' base.

Trrue bulbs multiply by producing at their platelike bases miniature bulbs—offsets—identical to their parent. In some hybrids, the parent bulb's vigor wanes after a season or two; growing offsets to flower or planting anew is the only way to keep such varieties in your garden. Harvest offsets as you lift your bulbs to increase their numbers, following these easy steps:

2 Remove and discard any of the small bulblets unless you plan to propagate them. They will usually take between two or three growing seasons to flower.

3 Discard any cut or damaged bulbs, along with those that show telltale signs of fungal decay such as white, powdery coating or soft, damp blemishes.

4 Allow the bulbs and offsets to dry thoroughly in a protected, well-ventilated, and shady spot with warm temperatures.

DIVIDING TUBERS AND RHIZOMES

Fleshy-rooted bulbous plants require division when their multiplant colonies become crowded. In general, lift and divide deciduous bulbs after flowering has finished and their foliage begins to wither. Divide evergreen bulbs in autumn or early spring. Divide bearded iris at early to midsummer. Gather a sharp, long-bladed knife, a shovel, two hand forks, gloves, and a tarp, then follow these easy steps:

1 Using a shovel, vertically cut the soil around the bulb colony, about 6–8 in. (15–20 cm) from the outermost stems.

2 Working with the shovel in a circular pattern outside the cut, remove soil with angled cuts to gain access to the soil beneath the colony.

3 Drive the shovel under the colony, freeing and lifting it. Set it onto a tarp.

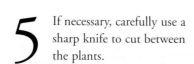

4 Use the two hand forks in opposition to one another, prying the colony apart and working between the plants.

5 If necessary, carefully use a sharp knife to cut between the plants.

6 Discard the oldest, central plants. Replant divided sets at the spacing recommended for the particular species.

CURING AND STORING BULBS

1 Cure the bulbs on a tarp or burlap in a dry, protected, well-ventilated, shady location with moderately warm temperatures for 10–14 days.

Storing bulbs while they are dormant until the proper planting time requires two steps: curing and the storage itself. Curing completes the process of lifting and ensures that the bulb enters dormancy. Storage conditions depend on the specific bulb type: either in an airy, dry location, or packed in slightly moist peat. Check the required storage conditions for each species of bulb [see Encyclopedia of Bulbous Plants, pg. 95]. Gather a tarp or burlap sack, soft brush, onion sacks, peat, and a breathable storage container, and follow these steps:

2 Remove withered foliage and clinging roots, and brush away any remaining soil. For bulbs with onionskin-like tunics, loosely pack them in a net bag or an open basket of dry peat.

THE RIGHT CONDITIONS

After bulbs are lifted from the garden, those with tunics should be cleaned and cured in a shady, warm, dry location with good air circulation. A temperature of 70–75°F (21–24°C) with low humidity is right for most tunicate bulbs. In 3–4 weeks, any remaining foliage will shrivel. It should be detached and discarded. This curing process helps harden the bulbs and prevents any lingering fungus spores from reproducing.

Divide and place the bulbs into cloth or net sacks, and hang them in a dry, dark location. For storage, most bulbs require 45–50°F (7–10°C) and humidity of 25 percent or less, as in an unheated garage. Run your hand through the bulbs every few weeks to rotate them, checking and removing any that have softened.

Beginning about 2 months before planting, chill the bulbs in a cold, humid space. An option is to put the bulbs into a loose paper sack with plenty of airholes and store them in your refrigerator's vegetable keeper.

Bulbs lacking tunicates are subject to drying, as are some summer-flowering bulbs and those of tropical origin. Dust these bulbs of clinging soil, set them in a bed of slightly moist peat or sawdust, and completely cover them with additional moist peat or sawdust. Store them at around 40°F (4°C), occasionally mixing and moistening the sawdust to keep them from dehydrating.

3 For dahlia, flag iris, and other easily dehydrated bulbs, loosely pack them in a porous container of barely moist peat.

4 Store the bulbs under the light, humidity, and temperature conditions each species requires.

ADVANCED TECHNIQUES

The propagation of bulbs includes techniques besides lifting, culturing offsets, and dividing roots. Some methods are suited to all bulbs, while others are unique to a specific species. They include removing and rooting cuttings from tuberous begonia and dahlia, harvesting and planting bulbils from lily and ornamental onion, removing cormels from gladiolus, rearing bulblets from narcissus and tulip, scoring hyacinth bulbs to ecourage new bulblets to grow, and scaling lilies. In addition, there are technical methods such as meristem and tissue culture. The easiest of these specialized techniques to master are taking cuttings and rearing bulbils or bulblets to flowering size [see How to Propagate Bulbs, next pg.].

Separating gladiolus cormels and rearing them should be done shortly after the parent plant's foliage has dried. Lift the old, dried corm and separate the new corms. Store them where they will receive good air circulation, at a temperature of 45–50°F (7–10°C), then plant them in the spring. The largest corms will flower the first season, but small ones may require two seasons or more to reach flowering size.

Scoring is a technique used to propagate hyacinths. Wearing rubber gloves to protect from skin irritation and using a sharp knife, carefully make a series of shallow cuts in a crisscross pattern into the bulb's basal plate, then plant the bulb as usual. After the foliage withers, you'll find small bulblets along the edge of the cuts. Harvest and rear them as with other bulblets.

Scaling lilies to produce new plants is best done with a sharp eye and a steady hand. Each scale must be removed with a small portion of its basal plate attached. Use a sharp knife to cut the scale away, and tweezers to gently detach it.

Scale lilies by carefully removing several outer scales containing a bit of the basal plate from the largest bulbs, then setting them in a mixture of half potting soil and half sand, leaving the top exposed. They will form bulblets along their bottom edge. Grow them as you would other bulblets. You'll have mature plants after about three seasons.

HOW TO PROPAGATE BULBS

Propagating bulbs from cuttings or by growing small offsets and bulbils to flowering size are popular ways to increase the number of your plants. Understanding and mastering these processes require time, patience, and practice. To root dahlia and tuberous begonia cuttings, you'll need loose, moist soil in a deep container and a sharp budding knife. To plant bulbils and bulblets, you'll need a hand trowel. Experiment with these advanced techniques by following these steps:

Cuttings

1 Begin by planting tubers of dahlia or begonia in containers, then keep them at 65°F (18°C) until they send up shoots.

2 When shoots are 3–5 in. (75–125 mm) long, cut them from the stem of the parent with a sharp budding knife.

3 Root them in damp potting soil or very sandy mix in a light spot. Cover with clear plastic to retain moisture, and keep warmer than 55°F (12°C). Avoid any foliage touching soil or plastic covering.

4 In 10–14 days, the cuttings will root. Repot them into an individual container.

Bulbils and Bulblets

1 Harvest small bulbils from the leaf axils of some lilies and ornamental onion, or collect bulblets from lifted bulbs.

2 In a bedding tray filled with moist potting soil, plant the single bulbils or bulblets ½ in. (12 mm) deep.

3 Lift and store the young plants after they yellow and wither. Plant them the following season about a quarter the depth of mature bulbs. Most will bloom in the third year.

Make growing
bulbs an all-year
hobby that
adds color to
your winter
home as you
learn forcing
techniques

Indoor Bulbs and Forcing

Can springtime be far behind when melting snow is the backdrop for the blooms of your colorful bulbs growing indoors? Here, paperwhite narcissus and tropical florist's amaryllis have been forced to flower months before their customary bloom season.

One of the most delightful midwinter treats you can enjoy is filling your home with aromatic and colorful blooming bulbs. Nearly a third of all the bulbs grown each year are reared for florists that sell forced flowers—bulbs grown out of season by following a series of steps easily copied in your home.

The most popular bulbs for indoor use are forced spring species: crocus, daffodil, hyacinth, iris, paperwhite, and tulip. Expand this group by including summer bulbs—cyclamen and lily, for instance—or evergreen and tropical species: amaryllis, tuberous begonia, and perennial ginger, among others.

Because bulbs store nutrients necessary for growth before they enter dormancy, they can sprout, shoot, and bloom with little more than water to sustain them. Such bulbs are exhausted by the experience, however; they should be discarded once their bloom finishes. If you wish to keep them, plant them in soil after their bloom and nurture them for a season or two until they regain their strength and begin to flower on their normal cycle.

Bulbs also can be forced indoors in soil in containers. When their bloom has faded, move them to the garden or a warm indoor location, then lift and store them as you would other bulbs. Blooming may be irregular for a season or two until they adjust.

Besides spring and summer bloomers, coax evergreen and tropical bulbs into bloom more than once a year; florist's amaryllis, for example, can produce two bloom cycles per year provided it is allowed to restore nutrients within its bulb. Use evergreens as houseplants in sunny sites and enjoy their beautiful flowers.

In this chapter, you'll be introduced to the care needed to force bulbs to grow when you want to display their flowers, shown a variety of techniques for growing bulbs indoors, told when to plant to have blooms for holiday parties or special events, and given tips on decorating with flowering bulbs grown indoors.

Create living floral displays in your home year-round with beautiful bulb plants, a great way to share your love of gardening with your family and friends.

GROWING BULBS INDOORS

Most bulbs grown indoors are tropicals and tender evergreen plants such as tuberous begonia, caladium, canna, clivia, and nerine, or spring and summer bulbs that you can force to bloom at your whim. Ample light, proper temperature, suitable preparation, and loving care are key to either group's success.

Tender bulbous plants naturally stem from regions of the world where weather conditions are mild to warm. They should be stored while semi-dormant in humid conditions at 40–50°F (4–10°C) depending on the species, held after planting for several weeks at 65°F (18°C) to grow roots, then moved to indirect sun at 68–72°F (20–22°C). Shelter them from overly dry air and direct air currents from home heating and air-conditioning vents, and mist them periodically when they become dry.

Tropicals tend to bloom in repeated cycles, while tender evergreens usually have only one bloom cycle per season of growth and dormancy. Divide them between flowerings whenever they become crowded or roots begin to emerge from their containers.

Forced spring and summer bulbs—crocus, daffodil, hyacinth, flag iris, Easter lily, paperwhite, and tulip, among others—are cured, stored, chilled, planted in soil or over water, and allowed to develop abundant roots and green shoots before they are moved to a bright, indoor location with normal room temperatures during the day and 55–60°F (13–16°C) at night [see Forcing Bulbs, pg. 88]. The total time needed is 6–16 weeks from chill until flowers open.

Some bulbs such as amaryllis can be planted without chilling; otherwise, their care is similar to that used for chilled spring and summer bulbs.

Give all your indoor bulbs bright, indirect sunlight—it limits their growth of foliage and stems. A south-facing window is an ideal location. At times when direct sunlight can create too-warm, drying conditions, place your bulbs near a light-colored wall in filtered sunlight.

Container plantings growing in an indoor garden can range from the simple but elegant pairing of tulips and lily-of-the-valley (right), to an island of vibrant color on a rustic plant stand. Note that this stand has been lined with galvanized sheet to waterproof it and simplify care.

PREPARING BULBS FOR FORCING

Spring bulbs need special preparation prior to planting if they will be forced. Because in nature they would winter through a cold, moist period followed by rapidly warming days, those conditions must be simulated artificially if they are to bloom. With practice, you will be able to entice bulbs to flower on cue. Gather your bulbs, dry sphagnum moss, and net bags or paper sacks with punched holes, and follow these simple steps:

1 Use either lifted, cured, and stored spring bulbs or those from your garden store, which may have been prechilled. Choose the largest possible bulbs to use for forcing.

2 If desired, make a base of sphagnum moss, then layer bulbs into the bag. Loosely close it, leaving air to circulate through punched holes.

GUIDE TO FORCING

Bulb	Chill*	Plant†	Bloomᐃ
Amaryllis (*Hippeastrum*)	None	65°F/18°C 3 weeks	68°F/20°C 3–4 weeks
Crocus	10 weeks	40°F/4°C 4–6 weeks	65°F/18°C 2–4 weeks
Daffodil	8 weeks	40°F/4°C 6–8 weeks	65°F/18°C 3–4 weeks
Hyacinth	63°F/17°C 8 weeks or more	40°F/4°C 6–8 weeks	70°F/21°C 2–3 weeks
Flag iris	5 weeks	40°F/4°C 6–8 weeks	68°F/20°C 3–4 weeks
Lily	6 weeks	40°F/4°C 6–8 weeks	65°F/18°F 8 weeks
Paperwhite	8 weeks	40°F/4°C 6–8 weeks	65°F/18°C 2–3 weeks
Tulip	8 weeks	40°F/4°C 4–6 weeks	65°F/18°C 4 weeks

Chill in the vegetable keeper of your refrigerator at 40–45°F (4–7°C) unless otherwise specified.

†*Time until shoots first emerge; confirm rooting has taken place, then move indoors to area with bright, indirect light.*

ᐃ*Bloom time varies with cultivar. Extend bloom period with cool overnight room temperature, 60–65°F (16–18°C).*

3 Unless they have been treated with fungicide, place the bag of bulbs into the humid vegetable keeper of a refrigerator; for treated bulbs, choose instead a sheltered indoor spot with similar temperature conditions. Chill them for at least the minimum number of weeks their species needs before planting in soil or suspending them above water in a bowl of rocks or hyacinth glass.

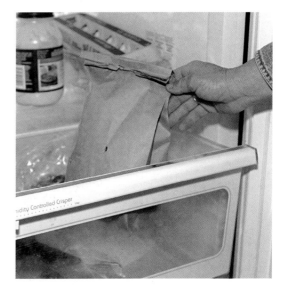

FORCING BULBS

Spring bulbs are the most commonly forced plants; only a few summer and evergreen bulbs are forced into bloom, usually so their flowering will match specific holiday occasions. You can force bulbs for display indoors in your home while outdoor conditions are still too cold to permit their growth, and you can force bulbs in your garden beds to match a special occasion such as a wedding or garden party. The general process to follow is easy to understand and master.

Forced spring and summer bulbs—crocus, daffodil, hyacinth, flag iris, Easter lily, paperwhite, and tulip, among others—are cured and stored depending on the species until 4–10 weeks before they are to be planted. Then they are chilled by keeping the unplanted bulbs in mildly humid conditions at 35–45°F (2–7°C). Following the chilling, they are planted in soil or suspended over water, then held in a low-light area at 50–65°F (10–18°C) until they develop abundant roots and green shoots. Finally, they are brought inside into a bright display location at 65°F (18°C) during the day and 55°F (13°C) at night, where they quickly grow foliage, develop flower shoots, and bloom. The total time needed is 12–20 weeks from beginning the chill until flowers [see Guide to Forcing, previous pg.]

Florist's amaryllis are best grown in soil. Obtained as bulbs from your garden center, planted in a container with sufficient depth and filled with quick-draining potting soil, the bulbs soon will sprout long, sword-shaped, fleshy leaves and a flower stalk. After their bloom is finished, move them to a warm spot and allow them to grow for another month, then reduce watering for 6–8 weeks to induce dormancy.

You can force your bulbs in water for an attractive, one-time display, or you can plant them in soil in containers or the garden. Each of these techniques is demonstrated here and in the pages that follow.

Forcing bulbs has been a gardening hobby for centuries; medieval tapestries and ancient frescoes depict forced bulbs blooming, sometimes in special crockery or glass vases. Blooming hyacinth in special hyacinth glasses became the vogue during Victorian times, and the pastime's popularity continues today [see Forcing Hyacinth, this pg.].

Achieving blooms for a specific time requires both planning and some experimentation. The precise control of bulb blooming times and growing plants out of phase with natural seasons is a technical subject that is best reserved for growers serving florists and specialized nurseries, but starting bulbs indoors for bloom in range of times is quite easily accomplished by any gardener that follows the required steps. Since bulbs are reared throughout the world before they are received by your garden retailer, you might be planting some bulbs grown in a different hemisphere with seasons reversed from those in your region. Other bulbs have been prechilled, heat-treated, or held under controlled conditions for varying, precise lengths of time, making them variable in their growth and bloom times.

For this reason it's best to set aside the largest bulbs lifted from your own garden for forcing if precision timing is your goal. Cure, store, chill, and plant several containers with a week's interval between them to ensure that you have top-quality blooms at the time you desire.

FORCING HYACINTH

Enjoy the fragrance of attractive and colorful hyacinths all winter long. In addition to single bulbs, hyacinths for forcing are offered in autumn as kits with hyacinth glasses.

Select large bulbs, heavy for their size. Seat the bulb in a hyacinth glass, pointed end up. Note the position of the base of the bulb, remove it, and fill the glass with water to a point just below the bulb's base, then set the bulb back in the glass.

Next put the glass into a dark, well-ventilated spot: a refrigerator, basement, or garage at 40–50°F (4–10°C). Avoid exposing the bulb to freezing temperatures. Check the water level every few days, and add more water when the level is too low.

In about 12 weeks, the bulb will fill the glass with roots and develop a shoot. Bring it indoors to a spot with indirect sunlight, 72°F (22°C). After the leaves expand, it should be moved to a warmer location until its growth accelerates.

When the foliage turns green, place it in full sunlight. It will bloom for 2–3 weeks.

FORCING BULBS IN WATER

Both clean, modern furnishings and rustic country decor match bulbs forced in a clear glass container partially filled with decorative rocks, polished stones, or marbles. Choose large, heavy bulbs for forcing; they'll need all of their nutrients to grow and bloom on water alone. Gather your container and polished stones or glass beads, and follow these easy steps:

1 In a clean medium-height container, make a bed of polished stones or glass beads at least as deep as the bulbs are tall.

2 Orient each bulb with its flat side to the pot and position it atop the stone bed. Nestle the bulbs down into the stones to hold them temporarily. Pack the bulbs tightly.

3 After each bulb is seated, fill the space between it and its neighbors with more stones.

4 Fill the container with water to slightly below the base of the bulbs. Chill them for the length of time recommended for the species.

FORCING BULBS IN SOIL

1 Cover the pot's drain hole with filter fabric or a piece of broken pot. Fill your container with potting soil at least 3 in. (75 mm) deep. Compact it.

Spring bulbs also can be planted in soil, either forced to bloom early or for bloom during their regular season. The best floral displays result when you crowd bulbs into the container. Large, firm bulbs have the largest blooms. Gather a container, potting soil, a trowel, gloves, and your bulbs, and follow these steps:

2 Tightly pack the bulbs in the container, orienting their tops upward and pressing them into the soil. Fill around the bulbs with potting soil.

3 Saturate the planting with water, then allow it to drain. If you force the bulbs, chill them for the recommended length of time for the species, keeping the soil damp until sprouts emerge.

FORCING AMARYLLIS

Florist's amaryllis—*Hippeastrum*—makes an attractive house-plant because of its showy blooms and glossy, spearlike foliage. An evergreen in mild-winter climates, amaryllis can be forced to bloom twice a year. You'll need a deep container, pea gravel, potting soil, a hand trowel, gloves, and a watering can. Follow these easy steps:

1 Shield the pot's drain hole from clogging by covering the bottom of the container with a layer of pea gravel, 1 in. (25 mm) deep.

2 Add potting soil, to 4 in. (10 cm) deep. Tamp it until firm to eliminate any air pockets.

3 Set the amaryllis bulb in the center, filling with soil to its shoulders and to the rim of the pot.

4 With your fingers, tamp the soil tightly around the bulb, until it is about 1 in. (25 mm) below the pot's rim.

5 Saturate the soil with water. Allow it to drain thoroughly. Set the pot in a shady spot at 65–70°F (18–21°C), and water to keep the soil barely moist until the bulb sprouts. Then place it in strong, indirect light to grow and bloom.

DECORATING WITH SPRING FLOWERS IN WINTER

Bulbs are a favorite for interior decorating because of their cheerful, bright colors, classic forms, and striking foliage unique among flowering plants. You might plant a cutting garden of bulbs in addition to those in your landscape. You also can force bulbs to flower during the winter and early spring [see Growing Bulbs Indoors, pg. 86]. Whichever choice you make, flower arrangements with bulbs and other growing plants will provide hours of enjoyment.

Consider wood sorrel for a March holiday; its shamrocklike leaves and tiny yellow flowers make it perfect for St. Patrick's Day. Brighten family holiday feasts with blooming lilies, florist's cyclamen, or florist's amaryllis. And create dainty table place settings with baskets of lily-of-the-valley and a centerpiece of bleeding heart.

Bulbs are well-suited to modern as well as traditional decor. Forced paperwhite narcissus, growing in water and smooth polished stones, suit the most elegant cut-crystal vase. Dainty corydalis can create feathery fernlike accents to contrast with a favorite Japanese bonsai sculpture in a miniature setting or to soften the stark beauty of Danish teak and cherry.

As a floral accent focus, massed spires of gladiolus and iris are tall, bright, and arresting. Scale your efforts to a smaller table by forcing grape hyacinth in a shallow container, or take advantage of rising steps to coordinate blooms at each level. Frame picture window views of the outdoors—and give your neighbors a treat—by placing matched vases of cut tulips and pussywillow to each side of its center.

(Right) Spruce up a cozy nook in your kitchen with a forced hyacinth and out-of-season fruit.

(Below) Add to festive holiday decorations by including tulips in a sculptural container with your other decorative touches.

Share your joy of gardening with your children or grandchildren by letting them plant a decoration for their room with your help. Try a dainty look in a girl's bedroom with a cheery pot of crocus, a dish of trillium, or a shower of snowflake. Boys may find ornamental onion's puffball seed heads fascinating.

There's a place for blooming bulbs in every room. A sewing nook brightens when you add a tuberous begonia above in a hanging planter. Bathroom counters and the humid regions near showers are perfect for such fragrant tropical evergreen bulbs as perennial ginger. Sunny kitchen windows will welcome the morning with crocus.

GROWING SUCCESSIONS OF FLOWERS INDOORS

Two options make it easy to grow successions of bulbs indoors. You either can grow different species of bulbs in several containers or grow mixed container plantings with bulbs that bloom at different times. Force bulbs in soil for individual plantings [see Forcing Bulbs in Soil, pg. 90]. Gather a large, deep container, a trio of bulbs with different bloom seasons and planting depths, pea gravel, potting soil, a hand trowel, and a watering can. Then follow these easy steps:

1 Cover the drain hole of the pot by lining the bottom with pea gravel. Then fill the pot with 3 in. (75 mm) of potting soil. Compact the soil.

2 Plant the largest, deepest species first. Crowd the bulbs into the pot. Then cover them to their neck with soil, pressing it to compact it.

3 Plant the next largest species, again crowding the bulbs in the container. Fill around them with soil until they are just covered.

4 Plant the smallest and shallowest species, again filling the container. Add soil to within 1 in. (25 mm) of the pot's rim.

5 Thoroughly water the pot, and place it in a protected spot outdoors or in an unheated, indoor location that will keep it safe from freezing temperatures.

6 When the bulbs sprout, move the container indoors into a spot with strong indirect light and temperatures of 65–70°F (18–21°C).

*G*ardeners who choose bulbs to plant in their landscape gardens or containers usually include one or more of everyone's long-time favorites such as crocus, daffodil, dahlia, daylily, hyacinth, gladiolus, iris, lily, or tulip. Besides these popular types, there are scores of other beautiful and fascinating bulbs.

The 87 bulbous plants featured on the following pages include true bulbs, corms, rhizomes, and tubers plus those with tuberous roots. Each is classified as a spring-, summer-, autumn-, or winter-planting type. Its season of bloom is given separately to help you pick the proper planting season for your area. Expanded descriptions and information are given for nine bulb families that are most frequently planted, along with example data for one or more members of each family.

This colorful encyclopedia is a visual identification guide as well as your source of accurate and timely information about the most widely planted bulbs found in home landscapes. When you admire bulbs that you see in a private or public garden near your home, compare them to the

> **Enjoy nature's bounty with a selection of striking bulbs suited to every region, season, landscape, and gardening purpose**

Encyclopedia of Bulbous Plants

The colorful world of bulbs includes such beautiful plants as (clockwise from top left) montebretia, a summer-blooming corm; lily-of-the-Nile, a summer-blooming rhizome; dahlia, a late summer-blooming tuberous root; and tulip, a spring-blooming true bulb that is a worldwide favorite.

photographs found here and use the information provided to decide how to use them to beautify your garden. The bulbs are listed by their most common name, followed by regional variations, then by their scientific name and family. Both common and scientific names are found in the index. Common names vary regionally—compare the common and scientific names to be sure the plant you acquire is really the one you want. There's a wealth of other descriptive information given for each plant, including its planting and bloom season; colors; habit; hardiness; complete spacing, depth, and care instructions; plus features that make it distinctive.

Use this encyclopedia as a guide to finding bulbs that will succeed in your garden. Check for plants well adapted to the conditions—the soil, sun, wind, and other climate factors—in your yard, bulb planting region, and plant hardiness [see Bulb Planting Regions, pg. 25, and USDA Plant Hardiness Around the World, pg. 132]. Note any special needs they may have for soil, light, watering, fertilizing, or post-bloom care.

Bulb: Amaryllis, Florist's. *Hippeastrum* hybrids. AMARYLLIDACEAE.
Description: Tropical bulb. Deciduous or evergreen. About 80 species. Stands 8–24 in. (20–60 cm) tall. Broad, straplike, arching, midlength green leaves.
Bloom: Winter–spring indoors, spring–summer outdoors. Orange, pink, red, white. One to five usually flared, trumpet-shaped, occasionally fragrant flowers 5–10 in. (13–25 cm) wide on a tall single or double stalk.
Plant hardiness: Zones 7–11. Ground hardy zones 9–10.
Soil: Well-drained. Fertility: Rich. 6.0–6.5 pH.
Planting: Autumn–winter in full sun. Space 1–2 ft. (30–60 cm) apart, slightly above soil level. In containers sized at least 2 in. (50 mm) wider than bulb, one bulb to a container, or several in very large containers.
Care: Easy. Keep moist early spring–autumn; avoid overwatering. Fertilize bimonthly until buds form. Deadhead flowers and withered stalks. Mulch. Propagate by offsets, seed. Allow bulbs to dry, cure for 1 month after lifting.
Storage: If deciduous, dark, 50–60°F (10–16°C), in net bag or open basket of dry peat moss; if evergreen, dark, 50–60°F (10–16°C), in porous container of dampened peat moss.
Features: Good choice for beds, bouquets, containers in cutting, indoor, tropical gardens. Good garden gift. Deer and rodent susceptible.

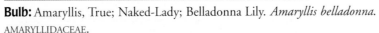

Bulb: Amaryllis, True; Naked-Lady; Belladonna Lily. *Amaryllis belladonna.* AMARYLLIDACEAE.
Description: Summer bulb. Deciduous. Stands 2–3 ft. (60–90 cm) tall. Straplike, midlength dull green leaves in clumps appear after flowers.
Bloom: Late summer–early autumn. Pink, red, white. Multiple flared, trumpet-shaped, fragrant flowers 3–4 in. (75–100 mm) wide on a tall, reddish stalk.
Plant hardiness: Zones 6–11. Ground hardy zones 8–11.
Soil: Well-drained humus. Fertility: Rich. 6.0–6.5 pH.
Planting: Late spring–early summer in full sun. Space 8–12 in. (20–30 cm) apart, at soil level. In containers, slightly above soil level.
Care: Moderate. Keep moist midsummer–early spring. Fertilize until buds form. Propagate by offsets. Divide only when crowded.
Storage: Dark, 55–70°F (13–21°C), in net bag or open basket of dry peat moss.
Features: Good choice for beds, borders, containers, cutting in cottage, indoor, tropical gardens. Deer, rodent resistant.

Bulb: Aztec Lily; Jacobean Lily. *Sprekelia formosissima.* AMARYLLIDACEAE.
Description: Summer bulb. Deciduous or evergreen. Stands 12–16 in. (30–40 cm) tall. Narrow, straplike, long, dark green leaves.
Bloom: Late spring–early summer. Red. Usually solitary, orchidlike flowers, 5–6 in. (13–15 cm) wide, on tall stalk.
Plant hardiness: Zones 8–11. Ground hardy zones 9–11.
Soil: Well-drained sandy loam. Fertility: Rich–average. 6.5–7.0 pH.
Planting: Spring in full sun. Space 6–12 in. (15–30 cm) apart, slightly below soil level.
Care: Moderate. Keep moist summer–spring. Fertilize until buds form. Protect from frost, zones 8–9. Propagate by bulbils, division, seed.
Storage: Dark, 50–60°F (10–16°C), in net bag or open basket of dry peat moss.
Features: Good choice for beds, borders, bouquets, containers, mass plantings in cottage, indoor, tropical gardens and landscapes. Spider mite susceptible.

Bulb: Baboon Flower. *Babiana* species. IRIDACEAE.
Description: Spring or summer corm, depending on species. Deciduous. About 61 species. Stands 6–12 in. (15–30 cm) tall. Straplike, short, hairy green leaves.
Bloom: Late spring–early summer. Blue, purple, red, violet, white, yellow. Multiple upright, star-shaped, often fragrant flowers 1–2 in. (25–50 mm) wide.
Plant hardiness: Zones 8–10. Ground hardy zones 9–10.
Soil: Well-drained sandy loam. Fertility: Average. 6.0–6.5 pH.
Planting: Autumn in full sun to partial shade, zones 9–10; spring, zone 8. Space 2–6 in. (50–150 mm) apart, 2–6 in. (50–150 mm) deep, depending on species. In indoor containers, space 1 in. (25 mm) apart, 1 in. (25 mm) deep.
Care: Moderate. Keep moist autumn–early summer. Fertilize until buds form. Remove withered foliage. Protect from wind. Propagate by bulbils, seed. Divide only when crowded.
Storage: Dark, 50–60°F (10–16°C), in porous container of dampened peat moss.
Features: Good choice for beds, borders, containers, drifts, edgings in cottage, rock gardens. Naturalizes.

Bulb: Begonia, Hardy. *Begonia grandis*. BEGONIACEAE.
Description: Summer tuber. Deciduous. Stands 18–36 in. (45–90 cm) tall. Wing-shaped, short bronze green leaves with red-tinted veins.
Bloom: Midsummer–autumn. Pink, white. Many drooping, fragrant flowers, 1–1½ in. (25–38 mm) wide, in clusters.
Plant hardiness: Zones 6–9. Ground hardy zones 7–9.
Soil: Well-drained. Fertility: Rich. 6.0–6.5 pH.
Planting: Spring in partial shade, zones 6–8; autumn, zone 9. Space 8–10 in. (20–25 cm) apart, 4 in. (10 cm) deep. In containers, space 3–4 in. (75–100 mm) apart, ¼ in. (6 mm) deep.
Care: Easy. Keep moist spring–autumn. Fertilize monthly during growth. Pinch early foliage buds to promote bloom. Propagate by cutting tubers into sections, each with an eye, or by cuttings.
Storage: Dark, 50–60°F (10–16°C), in net bag or open basket of dry peat moss.
Features: Good choice for beds, borders, ground cover, mixed plantings in formal gardens and landscapes. Deer, rodent and slug, snail susceptible.

Bulb: Begonia, Tuberous. *Begonia* × *tuberhybrida*. BEGONIACEAE.
Description: Summer or autumn tuber, depending on hybrid. Deciduous. Stands or trails 1–3 ft. (30–90 cm) tall or long. Wing-shaped, short bronze green leaves with reddish veins.
Bloom: Summer–autumn. Orange, pink, purple, red, white, yellow, variegated. Multiple open single, double, or very double, sometimes fringed or ruffled, often fragrant flowers to 8 in. (20 cm) wide. Available in erect or cascading forms.
Plant hardiness: Zones 4–11. Ground hardy zones 7–11.
Soil: Well-drained. Fertility: Rich. 5.5–6.5 pH.
Planting: Spring in partial shade. Space 6–12 in. (15–30 cm) apart, at soil level.
Care: Moderate. Keep moist spring–autumn. Fertilize monthly year round. Mulch, zones 4–8. Protect from frost, zones 4–6; heat, zones 10–11. Propagate by cutting tubers into sections, each with an eye.
Storage: Dark, 40–50°F (4–10°C), in net bag or open basket of dry peat moss.
Features: Good choice for beds, borders, containers in indoor gardens and landscapes. Good in hanging baskets. Deer, rodent and slug, snail susceptible.

Bulb: Blackberry Lily; Leopard Flower. *Belamcanda chinensis.* IRIDACEAE.

Description: Summer rhizome. Deciduous. Stands 2–4 ft. (60–120 cm) tall. Narrow, swordlike, upright or arching, long green leaves.

Bloom: Late summer–early autumn. Orange speckled with red. Multiple open, star-shaped flowers 2–3 in. (50–75 mm) wide form black berrylike clustered seed in autumn.

Plant hardiness: Zones 5–10. Ground hardy zones 8–10.

Soil: Well-drained sandy loam. Fertility: Rich–average. 6.5–7.0 pH.

Planting: Spring in full sun to partial shade. Space 10–12 in. (25–30 cm) apart, slightly below soil level.

Care: Easy. Keep moist during growth. Fertilize until buds form. Propagate by division in autumn, seed in spring. Best left undisturbed.

Storage: Dark, 50–60°F (10–16°C), in porous container of dampened peat moss.

Features: Good choice for borders in cottage gardens and landscapes. Dry berries for arrangements. Deer, rodent resistant. Mosaic virus susceptible.

Bulb: Blazing-Star; Gay-Feather. *Liatris* species. ASTERACEAE (COMPOSITAE).

Description: Summer corm or rhizome. Deciduous. About 35 species. Stands 2–5 ft. (60–152 cm) tall. Needlelike, linear, short, hairy green leaves in tiers along a spiked column. Cultivars include 'Floristan White', to 3 ft. (90 cm) tall; 'Kobold', a pink- to light purple; and 'Silvertips', with white-fringed flowers.

Bloom: Late summer–autumn. Purple, white. Multiple tiny flowerlike bracts in a feathery plume 12 in. (30 cm) long in tiers along stalk. Showy blooms open from top to bottom.

Plant hardiness: Zones 3–10. Ground hardy zones 4–9, depending on species.

Soil: Well-drained. Fertility: Average. 6.0–7.5 pH.

Planting: Spring in full sun. Space 6–8 in. (15–20 cm) apart, 1 in. (25 mm) deep.

Care: Easy. Keep moist spring–summer. Fertilize until buds form. Deadhead withered stalks. Mulch, zones 3–4. Protect from wind. Stake to support. Propagate by cormels, division in autumn, seed in spring.

Storage: Dark, 50–60°F (10–16°C), in porous container of dampened peat moss.

Features: Good choice for beds, borders, mixed plantings in butterfly, meadow, natural gardens. Deer, rodent resistant.

Bulb: Blood Lily. *Scadoxus* species (*Haemanthus* species). AMARYLLIDACEAE.

Description: Spring bulb. Deciduous. About 9 species. Stands 1–2 ft. (30–60 cm) tall. Broad, long bright green leaves.

Bloom: Spring–summer. Coral, red, white. Multiple brushlike flowers 1 in. (25 mm) wide and long form clusters to 9 in. (23 cm) wide, with berrylike fruits.

Plant hardiness: Zones 8–11. Ground hardy zones 9–11.

Soil: Well-drained. Fertility: Rich. 5.5–6.5 pH.

Planting: Spring in full sun to partial shade. Space 12 in. (30 cm) apart, at soil level. Choose container with ample space for root growth.

Care: Moderate. Keep moist spring–summer. Fertilize until buds form. Protect from frost, zone 8. Propagate by offsets in spring.

Storage: Best left undisturbed. If lifted, dark, 50–60°F (10–16°C), in net bag or open basket of dry peat moss.

Features: Good choice for beds, bouquets, containers in cutting, patio gardens and landscapes. Rodent and mosaic virus, slug, snail susceptible.

Bulb: Bugle Lily; Watsonia. *Watsonia* species. IRIDACEAE.

Description: Spring corm. Deciduous or evergreen. About 52 species. Stands 18–72 in. (45–180 cm) tall. Narrow, swordlike, short to long green leaves.

Bloom: Early spring–summer. Apricot, pink, purple, red, white. Multiple flared, trumpet-shaped, fragrant flowers 1½–3 in. (38–75 mm) long in tiers ascending vertically along stalk.

Plant hardiness: Zones 7–11. Ground hardy zones 9–11.

Soil: Well-drained. Fertility: Average. 6.0–6.5 pH.

Planting: Early autumn in full sun, zones 9–11; spring, zones 7–8. Space 6–9 in. (15–23 cm) apart, 3–4 in. (75–100 mm) deep.

Care: Easy. Keep moist spring–summer. Fertilize until buds form. Mulch. Propagate by cormels.

Storage: Dark, 50–60°F (10–16°C), in porous container of dampened peat moss.

Features: Good choice for beds, bouquets, containers in cutting gardens and landscapes. Naturalizes. Deer, rodent susceptible.

Bulb: Caladium, Fancy-Leaved; Elephant's-Ear. *Caladium × hortulanum* (*C. bicolor*). ARACEAE.

Description: Summer tuber. Deciduous. Stands 1–3 ft. (30–90 cm) tall. Broad, heart-shaped, short to long light green leaves 2–18 in. (5–45 cm) long, depending on hybrid, with pink, red, and white variegated patterns.

Bloom: Insignificant flowers; grown for foliage.

Plant hardiness: Zones 8–11. Ground hardy zones 9–11.

Soil: Well-drained. Fertility: Rich. 5.5–6.5 pH.

Planting: Late spring in partial shade to full shade. Space 12 in. (30 cm) apart, 1–3 in. (25–75 mm) deep.

Care: Moderate. Keep moist spring–autumn. Allow soil to dry when leaves wither. Fertilize until buds form. Protect from wind. Propagate by offsets.

Storage: Dark, 50–60°F (10–16°C), in net bag or open basket of dry peat moss.

Features: Good choice for borders, containers, edgings, mixed plantings in shade, tropical gardens. Good with annual and perennial flowers. Deer, rodent resistant.

Bulb: Calla Lily. *Zantedeschia* species. ARACEAE.

Description: Spring rhizome. Deciduous. About 6 species. Stands 1–4 ft. (30–120 cm) tall. Elongated heart-shaped, midlength, shiny dark green leaves, sometimes patterned with white speckles.

Bloom: Summer–autumn. Pink, red, white, yellow. Solitary petal-like spiral spathes form elegant flowers 4½–10 in. (11–25 cm) long.

Plant hardiness: Zones 8–10. Ground hardy zones 8–10.

Soil: Well-drained. Fertility: Rich. 6.0–7.0 pH.

Planting: Early autumn in full sun to partial shade. Space 12–16 in. (30–40 cm) apart, 4 in. (10 cm) deep.

Care: Easy. Keep damp at all times; may be placed in shallow water or garden pond margins. Fertilize bimonthly during growth. Mulch. Propagate by division, offsets, seed.

Storage: Dark, 50–60°F (10–16°C), in net bag or open basket of dry peat moss.

Features: Good choice for borders, bouquets, containers in cutting, indoor gardens and landscapes. Deer, rodent resistant. Spider mite susceptible.

Bulb: Camass. *Camassia* species. LILIACEAE.

Description: Spring bulb. Deciduous. About 5 species. Stands 30–48 in. (75–120 cm) tall. Narrow, straplike, long green leaves.

Bloom: Late spring. Blue, purple, white. Multiple star-shaped, sometimes lightly fragrant flowers 1–2 in. (25–50 mm) wide in tiers vertically along stalk.

Plant hardiness: Zones 3–9. Ground hardy zones 5–9.

Soil: Well-drained moist humus. Fertility: Rich–average. 6.0–6.5 pH.

Planting: Early autumn in full sun to partial shade. Space 6–10 in. (15–25 cm) apart, 4–6 in. (10–15 cm) deep.

Care: Easy. Keep moist spring–summer. Fertilize in spring. Propagate by division, seed. Best left undisturbed.

Storage: Dark, 50–60°F (10–16°C), in porous container of dampened peat moss.

Features: Good choice for beds, borders, bouquets, ground covers, mixed plantings in cutting, meadow, woodland gardens and water features. Naturalizes. Deer, rodent susceptible.

> **Warning**
>
> All parts of camass are hazardous if ingested. Avoid planting in areas frequented by children or pets.

Bulb: Canna; Indian-Shot. *Canna* hybrids. CANNACEAE.

Description: Summer rhizome. Semi-evergreen. About 9 species. Stands 4–16 ft. (1.2–4.9 m) tall. Showy wide, large, long, bronze, green, purple, red, white, yellow leaves with variegated patterns, sometimes fringed.

Bloom: Summer–autumn. Orange, pink, red, white, yellow, bicolor. Multiple clustered terminal, repeat-blooming flowers to 6 in. (15 cm) wide.

Plant hardiness: Zones 3–11. Ground hardy zones 7–11.

Soil: Well-drained. Fertility: Rich. 6.0–7.0 pH.

Planting: Autumn in full sun, zones 7–11; spring, zones 3–6. Space 1–2 ft. (30–60 cm) apart, slightly below soil level.

Care: Easy. Keep moist spring–early autumn. Fertilize until buds form. Deadhead flowers. Mulch. Protect from frost, zones 3–6. Propagate by division.

Storage: Dark, 50–60°F (10–16°C), in net bag or open basket of dry peat moss.

Features: Good choice for accents, borders, containers in tropical gardens and landscapes. Attracts hummingbirds. Slug, snail susceptible.

Bulb: Cape Cowslip; Leopard Lily. *Lachenalia* species. LILIACEAE.

Description: Spring bulb. Deciduous. About 90 species. Stands 6–16 in. (15–40 cm) tall. Straplike, double, short to midlength green leaves, sometimes patterned with spots.

Bloom: Late winter–early spring. Blue, pink, red, white, yellow, often edged in green, red, purple. Multiple cylinder-shaped flowers to 1½ in. (38 mm) long in tiers vertically along a single stalk.

Plant hardiness: Zones 8–10. Ground hardy zones 9–10.

Soil: Well-drained sandy loam. Fertility: Rich. 6.0–6.5 pH.

Planting: Autumn in full sun, zones 9–10; spring, zone 8. Space 4–6 in. (10–15 cm) apart, 2–3 in. (50–75 mm) deep.

Care: Easy. Keep moist autumn–spring. Fertilize until buds form. Deadhead flowers. Protect from frost, zone 8; sun in hot climates. Propagate by bulbils, seed. Prolong bloom by placing containers in a cool location at night.

Storage: Dark, 50–60°F (10–16°C), in net bag or open basket of dry peat moss.

Features: Good choice for beds, borders, bouquets, containers in cutting, indoor, rock gardens. Popular indoor houseplant. Slug, snail susceptible.

Bulb: Corn Lily. *Ixia* species. IRIDACEAE.

Description: Spring corm. Deciduous. About 30 species. Stands 6–36 in. (15–90 cm) tall. Grasslike, short to long bright green leaves.

Bloom: Late spring–summer. Orange, pink, red, white, yellow. Multiple open, six-petaled, sometimes fragrant flowers ½–1½ in. (12–38 mm) wide, with dark, contrasting centers, in dense spikes.

Plant hardiness: Zones 4–10. Ground hardy zones 7–9.

Soil: Well-drained. Fertility: Average. 6.5–7.0 pH.

Planting: Autumn in full sun, zones 9–10; spring, zones 4–8. Space 3–4 in. (75–100 mm) apart, 2–3 in. (50–75 mm) deep.

Care: Easy. Keep soil moist during growth. Fertilize until buds form. Mulch, zones 7–8. Lift, zones 4–6. Propagate by cormels in autumn, seed in spring.

Storage: Dark, 50–60°F (10–16°C), in porous container of dampened peat moss or in pot of dry soil.

Features: Good choice for beds, borders, bouquets, containers, drifts, mixed plantings in cottage, cutting, natural, small-space gardens and landscapes. Naturalizes.

Bulb: Crocus. *Crocus* species. IRIDACEAE.

Description: Spring corm. Deciduous. About 80 species. Stands 3–6 in. (75–150 mm) tall. Grasslike, short dark green leaves.

Bloom: Autumn or late winter–early spring, depending on species. Purple, white, yellow, striped. Solitary cup-shaped, sometimes fragrant flowers 1½–3 in. (38–75 mm) long appear stemless.

Plant hardiness: Zones 3–10. Ground hardy zones 4–8.

Soil: Well-drained. Fertility: Average. 5.0–6.5 pH.

Planting: Autumn in full sun to partial shade. Space 1–3 in. (25–75 mm) apart, 3–5 in. (75–125 mm) deep.

Care: Easy. Keep moist winter–spring. Fertilize when shoots appear. Mulch, zones 9–10. Propagate by division in autumn. Transplant container plants to garden in second year. Divide only when crowded.

Storage: Dark, 40–50°F (4–10°C), in net bag or open basket of dry peat moss.

Features: Good choice for beds, containers, edgings, mass plantings in cottage, meadow, woodland gardens. Naturalizes. Deer, rodent susceptible.

Bulb: Cyclamen, Florist's; Persian Violet. *Cyclamen persicum.* PRIMULACEAE.

Description: Spring tuber. Deciduous. Stands to 8 in. (20 cm) tall. Heart-shaped, mostly finely toothed, short green leaves, often marbled or veined with contrasting colors.

Bloom: Winter–spring. Pink, purple, red, white. Multiple shooting-star-shaped, often fragrant flowers to 2 in. (50 mm) long.

Plant hardiness: Zones 9–11. Ground hardy zones 9–10.

Soil: Well-drained. Fertility: Rich. 6.0–6.5 pH.

Planting: Autumn in partial shade to full shade. Space transplants 4–6 in. (10–15 cm) apart, slightly above soil level.

Care: Easy. Keep moist autumn–spring. Fertilize monthly during growth; dilute fertilizer to half the recommended rate. Mulch. Avoid disturbing roots. Propagate by division, seed.

Storage: Dark, 60–70°F (16–21°C), in pot of dry–slightly damp soil.

Features: Good choice for bed, border, containers, drifts in indoor, rock, shade, wildflower, woodland gardens. Good garden gift. Naturalizes.

DAFFODIL AND NARCISSUS

After tulips, members of the 26-species *Narcissus* genus are the second most popularly planted spring bulbs, and many thousands of hybrid cultivars have been registered. Most are native to Europe and North Africa. In common usage, daffodils have large blooms as compared to the often clustered and smaller-flowered narcissus. Jonquil, *N. jonquilla*, is another popular narcissus species. All narcissus are true, tunicate bulbs.

Most daffodils and narcissus are hardy, divide readily, and are easily propagated. Narcissus are divided into three subgenera—*Ajax, Corbularia,* and *Narcissus*—and six sections—*Jonquilleae, Ganymedes, Serotini, Hermione, Narcissus,* and × *Queltia*—as well as into 12 commonly recognized divisions:

I. Trumpet Narcissus	VII. Jonquilla Narcissus
II. Large-Cupped Narcissus	VIII. Tazetta Narcissus
III. Small-Cupped Narcissus	IX. Poeticus Narcissus
IV. Double Narcissus	X. Species and Wild-Hybrid Narcissus
V. Triandrus Narcissus	XI. Split-Corona Narcissus
VI. Cyclamineus Narcissus	XII. Other Narcissus

The divisions use such criteria as flower number, size, proportion, petal or corona arrangement, and color to distinguish between the many narcissus cultivars available, and are the basis for award categories in flower competitions. Classification terminology and registration of cultivar names is governed by the American Daffodil Society in the United States and by the Royal Horticultural Society in Britain.

Daffodil, narcissus, and jonquil usually are planted in autumn as soil temperatures cool, remain in the ground over the winter, and bloom in the spring. They can be planted in a variety of garden sites, including beds and borders, or naturalized beneath grass or as part of a rock garden. Their blooms last longest when they are planted in partially sunny locations with cool temperatures. Massed plantings of narcissus in open landscapes and turfgrass are especially colorful.

Bulb: Daffodil. *Narcissus* species. AMARYLLIDACEAE.

Description: Spring bulb. Deciduous. About 50 species, many hybrids. Stands 4–24 in. (10–60 cm) tall. Narrow, flat, straplike, light to dark green leaves.

Bloom: Late winter–early spring. Cream, orange, peach, pink, red, white, yellow, bicolored. Solitary or clustered trumpet-shaped, sometimes fragrant flowers ½–2 in. (12–50 mm) wide, with short to long, smooth or ruffled crowns, surrounded by single or double, sometimes frilly petals.

Plant hardiness: Zones 3–9. Ground hardy zones 4–9.

Soil: Well-drained to moist. Fertility: Rich–average. 5.5–6.5 pH.

Planting: Autumn in full sun to partial shade. Space 3–5 in. (75–125 mm) apart, 5–8 in. (13–20 cm) deep.

Care: Easy. Keep moist winter–spring. Fertilize until buds form. Propagate by division, offsets in autumn. Divide only when crowded.

Storage: Dark, 40–50°F (4–10°C), in net bag or open basket of dry peat moss.

Features: Good choice for borders, containers, drifts, mass plantings in cottage, cutting, meadow, woodland gardens. Naturalizes. Narcissus bulb fly susceptible; discard infested bulbs. Deer, rodent resistant.

DAHLIA

The roughly 27 wild species of the *Dahlia* genus native to Mexico and Central and northern South America have yielded more than 20,000 hybrid cultivars in a wide range of sizes, colors, and flower forms. All are summer bloomers, have tuberous roots, and are tender; dahlia are planted as annuals in USDA Plant Hardiness Zones 4–8, or are lifted after bloom and stored for spring replanting.

Dahlia are popular competition flowers and are divided for award purposes into 15 commonly recognized groups:

1. Single Dahlia
2. Anemone Dahlia
3. Collarette Dahlia
4. Peony Dahlia
5. Formal Decorative Dahlia
6. Informal Decorative Dahlia
7. Orchid-Flowering Dahlia
8. Ball Dahlia
9. Pompon Dahlia
10. Incurved Cactus Dahlia
11. Straight Cactus Dahlia
12. Semi-Cactus Dahlia
13. Miscellaneous Dahlia
14. Fimbriated Dahlia
15. Waterlily or Nymphaea-Flowered Dahlia

Classification is an active sport for dahlia enthusiasts, and a current listing of official categories may be obtained from the American Dahlia Society.

Dahlia usually are planted in spring as soon as soil temperatures have warmed, after several weeks with minimum nighttime air temperatures above 60°F (16°C). For USDA Plant Hardiness Zones 9–11, plant in autumn. They are long-lasting, summer-blooming flowers that frequently extend their showy bloom into autumn. Lift them after their blooms fade for storage and replanting.

Choose dahlia cultivars according to your planned use. Small varieties, to 2 ft. (60 cm) tall, are best used as edgings, bedding plants, and borders. Massed plantings of taller forms make an eye-catching landscape feature suitable for island beds, fenced gardens, or raised beds separated by winding paths.

Bulb: Dahlia. *Dahlia* hybrids. ASTERACEAE (COMPOSITAE).

Description: Summer tuberous root. Deciduous. Stands to 15 ft. (4.6 m) tall. Swirl of two or three simple, medium-toothed, short to midlength dark green leaves.

Bloom: Summer–autumn. Bronze, orange, pink, purple, red, white, yellow, bi- or multicolored. Multiple flowers to 12 in. (30 cm) wide, with single or layered petals, in widely varied forms from simple or pom-pom to cactuslike.

Plant hardiness: Zones 4–11. Ground hardy zones 9–11.

Soil: Well-drained. Fertility: Rich. 6.5–7.0 pH.

Planting: Autumn in full sun, zones 9–11; spring, zones 4–8. Space 2–3 ft. (60–90 cm) apart, 6 in. (15 cm) deep. Space dwarf hybrids 10–12 in. (25–30 cm) apart, 4–5 in. (10–13 cm) deep.

Care: Moderate. Keep moist summer–autumn. Fertilize until buds form. Mulch. Pinch foliage buds when 1 ft. (30 cm) tall to promote bushy growth. Lift, zones 4–7. Stake to support. Propagate by division in spring.

Storage: Dark, 50–60°F (10–16°C), in net bag or open basket of dry peat moss.

Features: Good choice for accents, beds, borders, bouquets in cottage, cutting gardens and landscapes. Deer, rodent, slug, snail susceptible.

DAYLILY

The genus *Hemerocallis* comprises more than 15 species, all native to Europe and Asia. These lily relatives now number several thousand cultivars. All are summer or autumn bloomers, have fleshy, tuberlike, fibrous roots, and many are cold hardy when protected by a layer of mulch from freeze-thaw cycles that otherwise would damage their roots in cold-winter climates of USDA Plant Hardiness Zones 3–7.

Daylilies adapt well to most soil conditions and do best in sites with at least 6 hours of sun daily. They are good container plants, and they can serve many different landscape purposes: banks, beds, borders, ground covers, massed and mixed plantings, or in rock gardens.

A daylily's clustered, often fragrant blooms are carried on upright stalks that extend above its sword-shaped, arching leaves. The lilylike flowers open sequentially along the stalk from bottom to top over a period of 3–4 weeks, with each blossom lasting a single day. Cultivars have been developed with early, mid-season, or late blooms, allowing you to create a lasting floral display from early summer to early autumn.

While the hybrid cultivars change from season to season, the following listing gives several choices in each color tested by the All-American Daylily Selection Council:

Yellow or Gold:
'Bitsy' (2002*)	'Happy Returns'	'Lady Florence'
'Miss Victoria'	'Starstruck' (1998*)	'Yellow Landscape Supreme'

Orange:
'Gertrude Condon'	'Lady Lucille'	'Lady Melanie'
'Leebea Orange Crush' (2002*)	'Leprechauns Wealth'	'Rocket City'

Pink:
'Judith' (2002*)	'Lady Georgia'	'Lady Rose'
'Lullaby Baby' 2002*)	'Miss Tinkerbell'	'Strawberry Candy'

Red:
'Lady Scarlet'	'Little Joy'	'Pardon Me'

Bicolored:
'Black-Eyed Stella' (1994*)	'Lady Eva'	'Radiant Greeting'

*All-American Daylily Selection

Bulb: Daylily. *Hemerocallis* species. LILIACEAE.
Description: Summer tuberous root. Deciduous or evergreen. About 15 species. Stands to 6 ft. (1.8 m) tall. Narrow, swordlike, arching green leaves.
Bloom: Late spring–autumn. Orange, pink, purple, yellow. Multiple flared, trumpet-shaped, sometimes fragrant flowers to 6 in. (15 cm) wide, in clusters.
Plant hardiness: Zones 3–10. Ground hardy zones 3–10.
Soil: Well-drained. Fertility: Average–low. 5.0–7.0 pH.
Planting: Spring, zones 3–6 in full sun to partial shade; autumn, zones 7–10. Space 15–24 in. (38–60 cm) apart, slightly below soil level.
Care: Easy. Keep moist spring–summer. Avoid fertilizing. Mulch. Propagate by dividing root sections, each with a growth point.
Storage: Dark, 40–50°F (4–10°C), in porous container of dampened peat moss.
Features: Good choice for beds, borders in cottage gardens and landscapes. Disease, pest resistant. Deer, rodent susceptible.

Bulb: Dog-Tooth Violet; Trout Lily. *Erythronium* species. LILIACEAE.
Description: Spring corm. Deciduous. About 25 species. Stands 4–24 in. (10–60 cm) tall. Two tongue-shaped, short to midlength green leaves, often mottled with brown, purple, or white.
Bloom: Spring. Pink, purple, rose, white, yellow, sometimes with color contrasts. Solitary to many nodding, star-shaped flowers to 2 in. (50 mm) wide.
Plant hardiness: Zones 3–9. Ground hardy zones 5–9.
Soil: Well-drained. Fertility: Rich. 5.0–6.5 pH.
Planting: Early autumn in bright to filtered shade, zones 5–9; spring, zones 3–4. Space 6–8 in. (15–20 cm) apart, 3–4 in. (75–100 mm) deep.
Care: Moderate–challenging. Keep moist in spring. Fertilize annually in spring. Mulch. Propagate by division, seed. Best left undisturbed.
Storage: Dark, 50–60°F (10–16°C), in porous container of dampened peat moss.
Features: Good choice for beds, borders, drifts, edgings, mixed plantings in rock, shade, woodland gardens. Naturalizes, self-seeds.

Bulb: Dutchman's-Breeches. *Dicentra cucullaria.* FUMARIACEAE.
Description: Spring tuber. Deciduous. Stands to 10 in. (25 cm) tall. Feathery, deeply toothed, short light blue green leaves form a midheight bush.
Bloom: Spring–summer. White, often tipped in cream yellow. Multiple nodding, unique, pantaloon-shaped flowers to 2 in. (50 mm) long, in branching clusters.
Plant hardiness: Zones 3–10. Ground hardy zones 4–9.
Soil: Well-drained humus. Fertility: Rich. 5.5–6.5 pH.
Planting: Autumn in partial shade. Space 12–18 in. (30–45 cm) apart, 1–2 in. (25–50 mm) deep.
Care: Moderate. Keep moist during growth. Fertilize until buds form. Remove withered foliage. Mulch. Protect from heat. Propagate by division in autumn, seed in spring.
Storage: Dark, 50–70°F (10–21°C), in net bag or open basket of dry peat moss.
Features: Good choice for beds, borders in natural, rock gardens. Self-seeds. Disease resistant.

Bulb: Elephant's-Ear; Taro. *Colocasia esculenta.* ARACEAE.
Description: Summer tuber. Evergreen. Stands 3–7 ft. (1–2 m) tall. Exotic, broad, heart-shaped, long, velvety, green or deep blue green leaves, often with contrasting veins.
Bloom: Insignificant flowers; grown for foliage.
Plant hardiness: Zones 8–11. Ground hardy zones 8–11.
Soil: Well-drained. Fertility: Rich. 5.5–6.5 pH.
Planting: Late spring in partial shade. Space 2 ft. (60 cm) apart, 2–3 in. (50–75 mm) deep.
Care: Moderate. Keep very moist spring–summer. Fertilize monthly during growth. Mulch. Propagate by offsets.
Storage: Dark, 50–60°F (10–16°C), in net bag or open basket of dry peat moss.
Features: Good choice for accents, beds, borders in tropical gardens and landscapes. Deer, rodent resistant.

Warning

Foliage and roots of elephant's-ear are hazardous if ingested. Avoid planting in areas frequented by children or pets.

Bulb: Fire Lily; Miniature Amaryllis. *Cyrtanthus* species. AMARYLLIDACEAE.
Description: Summer bulb. Deciduous or evergreen. About 45 species.
Stands to 18 in. (45 cm) tall. Straplike, arching, long green leaves.
Species include Scarborough lily, *C. elatus*, and *C. mackenii.*
Bloom: Summer. Pink, red, white, yellow. Multiple flared, trumpet-
shaped, amaryllis-like, fragrant flowers 1–1½ in. (25–38 mm) long.
Plant hardiness: Zones 7–11. Ground hardy zones 9–11.
Soil: Well-drained humus. Fertility: Rich. 6.2–6.8 pH.
Planting: Spring in full sun to light shade. Space 6–12 in. (15–30 cm)
apart, with neck of bulb at soil level.
Care: Easy. Keep damp spring–summer; avoid overwatering. Reduce
watering after bloom. Fertilize until buds form. Protect from frost,
zones 7–9. Propagate by division, offsets, seed.
Storage: Dark, 55–65°F (13–18°C), in net bag or open basket of dry peat moss.
Features: Good choice for beds, borders, bouquets, containers in cottage, cutting, indoor
gardens and landscapes.

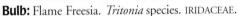

Bulb: Flame Freesia. *Tritonia* species. IRIDACEAE.
Description: Spring bulb. Deciduous. About 50 species. Stands to 18 in. (45 cm)
tall. Straplike, arching, midlength to long green leaves.
Bloom: Autumn–early summer. Orange, pink, red, white, yellow. Multiple cup-
shaped flowers 1–2 in. (25–50 mm) wide.
Plant hardiness: Zones 7–10. Ground hardy zones 9–10.
Soil: Well-drained. Fertility: Rich–average. 6.0–7.0 pH, depending on species.
Planting: Autumn in full sun, zones 9–10; spring, zones 7–8. Space 6–10 in.
(15–25 cm) apart, 3–4 in. (75–100 mm) deep.
Care: Easy. Keep moist autumn–early summer, dry in summer. Fertilize monthly
during growth. Mulch. Propagate by division.
Storage: Dark, 40–50°F (4–10°C), in net bag or open basket of dry peat moss.
Features: Good choice for beds, borders, bouquets, containers in cutting, indoor,
tropical gardens and landscapes. Naturalizes. Deer, rodent susceptible.

Bulb: Florist's Gloxinia. *Sinningia speciosa* hybrids (*Gloxinia speciosa*). GESNERIACEAE.
Description: Tropical tuber. Deciduous. Stands to 1 ft. (30 cm) tall. Oblong, finely
toothed, midlength hairy green leaves, often with reddish undersides.
Bloom: Year-round indoors, summer outdoors. Blue, orange, pink, purple, red,
white, yellow, often banded or speckled with color contrasts. One to two nodding,
funnel-shaped, sometimes ruffled flowers to 5 in. (13 cm) wide.
Plant hardiness: Zones 10–11. Ground hardy zones 10–11.
Soil: Well-drained humus. Fertility: Rich. 6.0–6.5 pH.
Planting: Early summer in partial shade, outdoors; indoors, year-round. Space
1 ft. (30 cm) apart, 1 in. (25 mm) deep. In containers sized at least 2 in. (50 mm)
wider than tuber, one to a container.
Care: Easy. Keep moist during growth. Fertilize monthly during growth. Mulch.
Protect from rain, wind. Propagate by cuttings, division, seed.
Storage: Dark, 60°F (16°C), in net bag or open basket of dry peat moss or pot of
barely damp soil.
Features: Good choice for beds, borders, containers in indoor, tropical gardens. Popular indoor
houseplant. Good garden gift.

Bulb: Freesia. *Freesia* species and hybrids. IRIDACEAE.
Description: Summer corm. Deciduous. About 19 species, many hybrids. Stands to 18 in. (45 cm) tall. Grasslike, midlength bright green leaves, in fans.
Bloom: Spring, zones 7–10; summer, zones 4–6. Blue, orange, pink, purple, red, white, yellow. Multiple flared, sometimes double, trumpet-shaped, fragrant flowers to 2 in. (50 mm) long, in linear, branching clusters.
Plant hardiness: Zones 4–10. Ground hardy zones 9–10.
Soil: Well-drained. Fertility: Rich–average. 6.5–7.5 pH.
Planting: Autumn in full sun, zones 9–10; spring, zones 7–8. Space 3–4 in. (75–100 mm) apart, 1–2 in. (25–50 mm) deep. Best planted annually in spring as new stock, zones 4–8.
Care: Moderate. Keep moist autumn–spring. Fertilize until buds form; dilute fertilizer to half the recommended rate. Deadhead. Mulch. Protect from wind. Stake to support. Propagate by offsets, seed.
Storage: Dark, 50–60°F (10–16°C), in net bag or open basket of dry peat moss.
Features: Good choice for beds, borders, bouquets, containers in cutting, indoor, cottage gardens and landscapes. Naturalizes.

Bulb: Fritillary; Checkered Lily. *Fritillaria meleagris.* LILIACEAE.
Description: Spring bulb. Deciduous. Stands 16 in. (40 cm) tall. Radiating, grasslike, midlength green leaves. Close relative of crown imperial, *F. imperialis*, with bare, stalks, radiating flowers and leafy crown.
Bloom: Spring. Brown, pink, purple, violet, white, with variegated geometric patterns. Multiple nodding, bell-shaped, musk-fragrant flowers 2–2$\frac{1}{2}$ in. (50–63 mm) long, in clusters.
Plant hardiness: Zones 2–9. Ground hardy zones 4–7.
Soil: Well-drained sandy loam. Fertility: Average. 6.0–7.5 pH.
Planting: Autumn in full sun to partial shade, zones 4–9; spring, zones 2–3. Space 6–8 in. (15–20 cm) apart, 4–8 in. (10–20 cm) deep.
Care: Easy–moderate. Keep moist in spring–summer. Fertilize in spring. Mulch in zones 8–9. Protect from heat. Propagate by offsets. Best left undisturbed.
Storage: Dark, 40–50°F (4–10°C), in net bag or open basket of dry peat moss.
Features: Good choice for accents, beds, borders in meadow, woodland gardens and landscapes. Deer, rodent resistant.

Bulb: Fumaria; Fumewort. *Corydalis* species. FUMARIACEAE.
Description: Spring rhizome or tuber. Deciduous. About 300 species. Stands 6–12 in. (15–30 cm) tall. Fernlike, midlength blue green leaves.
Bloom: Spring. Blue, pink, purple, red, white, yellow. Multiple nodding, tubelike flowers, $\frac{1}{2}$–1 in. (12–25 mm) long, in clusters.
Plant hardiness: Zones 4–8. Ground hardy zones 6–8.
Soil: Well-drained sandy loam. Fertility: Average. 6.0–8.0 pH.
Planting: Autumn in partial shade to full shade; spring for transplants. Space 3–6 in. (75–150 mm) apart, 2–4 in. (50–100 mm) deep.
Care: Easy. Keep moist in spring. Fertilize in spring. Mulch. Protect from heat. Propagate by division, seed.
Storage: Dark, 50–60°F (10–16°C), in porous container of dampened peat moss.
Features: Good choice for beds, borders in rock, shade, woodland gardens. Naturalizes, self-seeds. Deer and pest resistant.

GINGER

ZINGIBERACEAE is a diverse family of nearly 40 genera and thousands of species of tropical rhizomatous herbs, including true ginger, *Zingiber officinale*, from which the spice is obtained [see this pg.]. In addition, there are many colorful ornamental plants with fragrant blossoms that are ideal for indoor gardens and greenhouses in USDA Plant Hardiness Zones 4–9, or for landscape planting in zones 10–11.

The most popular ornamental gingers include:

Alpinia species, shell ginger or ginger lily: a landscape plant to 10 ft. (3 m) tall, with pink or white, nodding, clustered, bell-shaped flowers;

Curcuma species, hidden lily: a very tropical, upright and radiating, fan-shaped plant to 30 in. (75 cm) tall, with spikes of multiple orange or red, upturned, trumpet-shaped flowers;

Globba species, dancing lady ginger: a delicate and shrublike, broad-leafed plant to 2 ft. (60 cm) tall, with purple and yellow, nodding, branching, clustered flowers;

Hedychium species, ginger lily or butterfly ginger: a tropical landscape plant to 10 ft. (3 m) tall, in spreading colonies, each stalk bearing coral, orange, pink, white, or yellow orchidlike flowers with graceful stamens; and

Kaempferia species, peacock ginger: a colorfully patterned ground cover, to 18 in. (45 cm) tall, with lone, simple, blue or pink, four-petaled flowers on upright stalks.

Ginger should be planted in spring in rich, well-drained soil after temperatures are consistently over 60°F (16°C); in cooler climates, plant in containers and protect from lower temperatures. Keep the plants consistently moist during their active growth period, fertilizing at each watering with a liquid fertilizer diluted to half its recommended rate. After bloom, reduce watering for 4–8 weeks to help the plant become semi-dormant, then resume regular watering.

Ginger always should be protected from direct sunlight while given lots of bright, indirect light. During winter, supplemental lighting will extend the plant's growth and bloom periods. Prune to maintain compact growth, and divide when roots become crowded. Remember that ginger is invasive in landscape plantings.

Bulb: Ginger, True. *Zingiber officinale* hybrids. ZINGIBERACEAE.

Description: Summer rhizome. Deciduous or evergreen. Stands to 20 in. (50 cm) tall. Lancelike, midlength green leaves in tiers along stalk.

Bloom: Summer. Orange, pink, white, yellow, sometimes blended or edged with contrasts. Multiple trumpet-shaped, sometimes orchidlike flowers in upright or drooping spikes.

Plant hardiness: Zones 8–11. Ground hardy zones 9–11.

Soil: Well-drained. Fertility: Rich–average. 6.0–6.5 pH.

Planting: Spring in bright shade. Space 6–12 in. (15–30 cm) apart, 2–4 in. (50–100 mm) deep.

Care: Moderate. Keep moist during growth. Fertilize during growth. Mulch. Protect from frost, zones 8–9. Propagate by division in spring.

Storage: Dark, 60–65°F (16–18°C), in net bag or open basket of dry peat moss.

Features: Good choice for beds, borders, margins, mass plantings in tropical, woodland gardens, landscapes, and water features. Source of the cooking spice treasured for many dishes in Asian cuisine.

GLADIOLUS

The *Gladiolus* genus comprises as many as 300 species—few in cultivation—plus thousands of hybrids and cultivars, all native to the Mediterranean region of Europe, Africa, and the Middle East. All are spring- and summer-blooming, semi-hardy corms, planted in spring, lifted during autumn, divided, and stored for replanting in USDA Plant Hardiness Zones 3–6 or planted during autumn and allowed to overwinter beneath protective mulch in zones 7–11. Most available are hybrid grandiflora gladiolus.

Besides the large hybrid cultivars, several gladiolus groupings based on flower form and individual cultivated species exist, such as:

Baby or Miniature Gladiolus	Abyssinian Sword Lily, *G. callianthus*
Butterfly Gladiolus	Byzantine Gladiolus, *G. communis* var. *byzantinum*
Primrose Hybrid Gladiolus	Grecian Gladiolus, *G. illyricus*

Gladiolus are easily recognized in the landscape: prior to flowering, they are tall, statuesque plants with sword-shaped, deep green leaves. Beginning in late spring, a tall, canelike flower spike emerges from the center of the plant. Over several days, the flowers open from the bottom to the top of the spike, forming an exquisite, clustered, frequently frilled cascade in a variety of colors.

Plant them in beds or borders where they will be the central focus, or use them as edgings along fences, paths, or structures. If potted, choose large containers to allow them ample soil; regardless of use, plant them where they will receive at least 6 hours of full sunlight each day, except in zones 10–11, where the sun should be filtered.

When blooms dwindle, the spikes should be deadheaded while allowing the foliage to remain until it begins to dry. Cut the foliage back to the corm and lift or mulch over them, depending on climate.

Gladiolus are treasured for cut-flower arrangements. For best results, water plants thoroughly the evening before cutting. Prune young flower stalks with partially opened blossoms using clean, sharp bypass hand shears, and immediately immerse the cut end in a bucket of cold water. After all of the flowers have been harvested, cut their stems again under water to avoid air pockets in the cut stem.

Bulb: Gladiolus; Sword Lily; Corn Flag. *Gladiolus* species. IRIDACEAE.

Description: Summer corm. Deciduous. About 300 species, many hybrids. Stands 1–6 ft. (30–180 cm) tall. Narrow, swordlike, midlength to long green leaves.

Bloom: Spring, zones 7–11; summer, zones 3–6. Orange, pink, purple, red, white, yellow, multicolored, striped. Multiple upturned, flared, trumpet-shaped, often fragrant flowers 1–8 in. (25–200 mm) wide, in tiers along one side of stalk. Blooms open from bottom to top.

Plant hardiness: Zones 3–11. Ground hardy zones 7–11.

Soil: Well-drained sandy loam. Fertility: Rich–average. 6.0–6.5 pH.

Planting: Spring–early summer in full sun, zones 3–8; year-round, zones 9–11. Space 4–6 in. (10–15 cm) apart, 4–6 in. (10–15 cm) deep.

Care: Easy. Keep moist during growth. Fertilize until buds form. Mulch. Propagate by cormels, seed.

Storage: Dark, 50–60°F (10–16°C), in net bag or open basket of dry peat moss.

Features: Good choice for beds, borders, bouquets, containers in cottage, cutting, rock gardens and landscapes. Deer, rodent, and thrip susceptible.

Bulb: Glory-of-the-Snow. *Chionodoxa* species. LILIACEAE.

Description: Spring bulb. Deciduous. About 6 species. Stands 3–6 in. (75–150 mm) tall. Narrow, straight, short dark green leaves.

Bloom: Early spring–summer. Blue, pink, white, with white centers. Multiple six-pointed, star-shaped flowers to 1 in. (25 mm) wide, in tiers of six to ten flowers vertically along stalk.

Plant hardiness: Zones 3–8. Ground hardy zones 5–8.

Soil: Well-drained. Fertility: Average. 6.0–7.0 pH.

Planting: Autumn in full sun to partial shade. Space 2 in. (50 mm) apart, 4 in. (10 cm) deep.

Care: Easy. Keep moist autumn–spring, damp in summer. Fertilize until buds form. Mulch, zones 7–8. Protect from frost. Propagate by division, offsets, seed in autumn. Divide only when crowded.

Storage: Dark, 50–60°F (10–16°C), in net bag or open basket of dry peat moss.

Features: Good choice for borders, containers, mass plantings in cottage, meadow, rock, woodland gardens. Naturalizes. Endangered species.

Bulb: Gloxinia, True. *Gloxinia gymnostoma*. GESNERIACEAE.

Description: Summer rhizome. Evergreen. Stands to 2 ft. (60 cm) tall. Narrow, oval, arching, short, hairy, deep green leaves.

Bloom: Summer–early autumn. Pink, speckled with red. Solitary, elegant, pendulous, flared, funnel-shaped flowers to 1¾ in. (45 mm) long.

Plant hardiness: Zones 9–11. Ground hardy zones 10–11.

Soil: Well-drained. Fertility: Rich–average. 6.5–7.5 pH.

Planting: Spring in partial shade. Space 6–8 in. (15–20 cm) apart, 1–2 in. (25–50 mm) deep. In containers sized at least 2 in. (50 mm) wider than rhizome, one to a container.

Care: Easy. Keep moist year-round. Fertilize spring–autumn. Mulch. Propagate by division, offsets, seed.

Storage: Dark, 50–60°F (10–16°C), in net bag or open basket of dry peat moss.

Features: Good choice for beds, borders, containers in indoor, rock, tropical gardens and greenhouses.

Bulb: Grape Hyacinth. *Muscari* species. LILIACEAE.

Description: Spring bulb. Deciduous. About 40 species. Stands 4–12 in. (10–30 cm) tall. Straplike, short to midlength green leaves. Species include *M. armeniacum*, *M. azureum*, *M. comosum*, *M. latifolium*, and *M. neglectum*.

Bloom: Early spring. Blue, purple, white. Multiple tube-shaped fragrant flowers to ¼ in. (6 mm) long, in tiers ascending along stalk, form a cone-shaped cluster.

Plant hardiness: Zones 3–11. Ground hardy zones 5–9.

Soil: Well-drained sandy loam. Fertility: Average. 6.0–7.0 pH.

Planting: Autumn in full sun to partial shade. Space 4–6 in. (10–15 cm) apart, 2–3 in. (50–75 mm) deep.

Care: Easy. Keep moist in spring, dry in summer. Fertilize until buds form. Mulch. Propagate by offsets, seed.

Storage: Dark, 40–50°F (4–10°C), in net bag or open basket of dry peat moss.

Features: Good choice for beds, borders, bouquets, containers, drifts, edgings, mass plantings, mixed plantings in cutting, indoor, meadow, rock, woodland gardens. Naturalizes. Deer, rodent resistant.

Bulb: Habranthus; Rain Lily. *Habranthus* species. AMARYLLIDACEAE.
Description: Summer bulb. Tropical. About 10 species. Stands to 9 in. (23 cm) tall. Narrow, straplike, arching, midlength to long green leaves.
Bloom: Summer; may bloom again in autumn. Copper, pink, purple, red, white, yellow. Solitary or multiple flared, trumpet-shaped flowers to 3 in. (75 mm) wide.
Plant hardiness: Zones 8–11. Ground hardy zones 10–11.
Soil: Well-drained. Fertility: Average. 6.0–7.0 pH.
Planting: Spring in full sun to partial shade. Space 3–6 in. (75–150 mm) apart, 1–2 in. (25–50 mm) deep.
Care: Moderate. Keep moist in late spring, dry after bloom. In zones 9–11, resume watering after 4 weeks for repeat bloom. Fertilize during growth. Mulch. Propagate by offsets, seed.
Storage: Dark, 40–50°F (4–10°C), in net bag or open basket of dry peat moss.
Features: Good choice for beds, borders, containers in cottage, patio, rock gardens and landscapes.

Bulb: Hyacinth; Garden Hyacinth. *Hyacinthus orientalis.* LILIACEAE.
Description: Spring bulb. Deciduous. Stands to 1 ft. (30 cm) tall. Straplike, curved-edged, midlength green leaves.
Bloom: Spring. Apricot, blue, orange, pink, purple, red, white, yellow. Multiple flared, trumpet-shaped, fragrant flowers to 1 in. (25 mm) wide, in snug tiers vertically along the stalk, form cone-shaped plumes.
Plant hardiness: Zones 4–11. Ground hardy zones 6–9.
Soil: Well-drained sandy loam. Fertility: Rich. 5.0–6.5 pH.
Planting: Autumn in full sun to partial shade. Protect from sun in hot climates. Space 6–8 in. (15–20 cm) apart, 5–8 in. (13–20 cm) deep.
Care: Easy. Keep moist in spring. Fertilize until buds form. Mulch. Lift after bloom, zones 4–5 and 8–11. Propagate by offsets.
Storage: Dark, 40–50°F (4–10°C), in net bag or open basket of dry peat moss.
Features: Good choice for beds, borders, containers in cottage, indoor, woodland gardens. Naturalizes, depending on cultivar. Deer, rodent resistant.

Bulb: Iris, Blue Flag; Wild Iris. *Iris versicolor.* IRIDACEAE.
Description: Summer rhizome. Deciduous. Stands to 30 in. (75 cm) tall. Narrow, strap- or swordlike, upright or arching long midgreen leaves.
Bloom: Summer. Blue, lavender, white. Solitary or multiple, fleur-de-lis-shaped flowers to 3 in. (75 mm) wide with upright petals form drooping beardless falls.

Plant hardiness: Zones 2–9. Ground hardy zones 4–7.

> **Warning**
>
> Plant sap of blue flag iris can cause skin irritation in sensitive individuals. Wear gloves when handling or pruning bulbs.

Soil: Moist; in water margins, to 6 in. (15 cm) deep. Fertility: Average. 6.0–7.0 pH.
Planting: Autumn in full sun to partial shade. Space 1–2 ft. (30–60 cm) apart, 2–3 in. (50–75 mm) deep. Submerge to 6 in. (15 cm) deep.
Care: Easy. Keep moist year-round. Fertilize annually in spring. Mulch. Propagate by division in midsummer.
Storage: Dark, 40–50°F (4–10°C), in net bag or open basket of dry peat moss.
Features: Good choice for bouquets, edgings, foregrounds, mass plantings, water margins in cutting, rock, shade gardens and water features. Deer, rodent, and iris borer susceptible.

IRIS

About 200 species and many hybrid cultivars make up the genus *Iris*, mostly native to the northern temperate zone. The horticultural classification of iris is complex and has been subject to many changes over time. A current listing of official categories may be obtained from the American Iris Society.

In general, iris separate into the rhizomes, subgenus *Iris;* the true bulbs, subgenera *Xiphium* or *Scorpiris;* and a single-species subgenus with pseudo-rhizomatous roots, *Nepalenses.* The first two of these divisions contain most popular cultivated iris:

Rhizomatous Iris:
   Bearded Iris (*I.* × *germanica*)
   Crested Iris (*I. confusa, I. cristata, I. japonica, I. tectorum, I. wattii*)
   Beardless Iris: Japanese (*I. ensata*), Louisiana (*I. brevicaulis, I. fulva,*
      I. giganticaerulea, I. hexagona, I. pseudacorus), Pacific (*I. douglasiana,*
      I. innominata, I. versicolor), Siberian (*I. siberica, I. sanguinea*), and Spuria
      (*I. chrysographes, I. clarkei, I. delavayi, I. dykesii, I. forrestii, I. wilsonii*)
Bulb Iris:
   Reticulata Iris (*I. danfordiae, I. histrio, I. histrioides, I. reticulata*)
   Juno Iris (*I. albomarginata, I. aucheri, I. bucharica, I. caucasica, I. fosterana*)
   Dutch and Spanish Iris (*I.* × *tigitana, I. xiphium*)
   English Iris (*I. latifolia, I. xiphiodes*)

Plant rhizomatous iris in late summer or autumn, bulbous iris in autumn. A sunny spot is best, but most tolerate filtered, partial sun. Use iris for edgings, low foreground plantings in beds and borders and for featured mass plantings, or plant them in containers and along the shorelines of water features.

Iris, especially flag iris, are excellent cut flowers. Water the plants well the evening before, and choose partially opened spikes. Immerse the cut stems in cool water immediately after cutting, then trim them again underwater prior to arranging.

Bulb: Iris, Fan; False Flag; Walking Iris. *Neomarica* species. IRIDACEAE.
Description: Spring rhizome. Deciduous. About 15 species. Stands 1–3 ft. (30–90 cm) tall. Straplike, long green leaves, sometimes with variegated patterns. Species include *N. caerulea;* walking iris, *N. gracilis; N. longifolia;* and apostle plant, *N. northiana.*
Bloom: Spring–summer. Blue, white, yellow, often with blue, brown, purple, or yellow contrasts or markings at center. Multiple irislike, fragrant flowers to 4 in. (10 cm) wide, in clusters. Individual blooms appear in sequence, each lasting but a single day.
Plant hardiness: Zones 8–11. Ground hardy zones 9–11.
Soil: Well-drained. Fertility: Rich. 6.0–6.5 pH.
Planting: Spring in full sun to partial shade. Space 6–8 in. (15–20 cm) apart, slightly below soil level.
Care: Moderate. Keep moist spring–summer. Fertilize in spring. Deadhead withered stalks. Mulch. Propagate by division, offsets that root where flowering stems touch the soil.
Storage: Dark, 50–60°F (10–16°C), in porous container of dampened peat moss.
Features: Good choice for beds, borders, containers in indoor, tropical, woodland gardens. Deer, rodent susceptible.

Bulb: Iris, German Bearded. *Iris* × *germanica* hybrids. IRIDACEAE.

Description: Summer rhizome. Deciduous. Thousands of hybrids. Stands to 30 in. (75 cm) tall. Narrow, strap- or swordlike, upright or arching, long midgreen leaves. Most bearded iris hybrids derive from German iris, *I.* × *germanica.* Dwarf, miniature dwarf, and median hybrids available.

Bloom: Summer or repeat blooming in spring and autumn, depending on hybrid. Nearly all colors, bicolored, blends. Multiple, fleur-de-lis-shaped flowers to 3 in. (75 mm) wide with three upright and three nodding petals bearing drooping bearded falls, on succulent stalks.

Plant hardiness: Zones 4–10. Ground hardy zones 6–10.

Soil: Well-drained humus. Fertility: Average. 6.0–7.0 pH.

Planting: Autumn in full sun to partial shade, zones 8–10; late summer, zones 4–7. Space 1–2 ft. (30–60 cm) apart, 2–4 in. (50–100 mm) deep, or cluster odd number of plants 6 in. (15 cm) apart for mass color.

Care: Easy. Keep moist during growth; reduce watering after flower stalks dry. Fertilize in spring. Mulch. Propagate by division in summer, seed.

Storage: Dark, 40–50°F (4–10°C), in net bag or open basket of dry peat moss.

Features: Good choice for bouquets, edgings, foregrounds, mass plantings in cutting, shade gardens. Deer, rodent, and iris borer susceptible.

Bulb: Jack-in-the-Pulpit. *Arisaema triphyllum.* ARACEAE.

Description: Spring tuber. Deciduous. Stands to 2 ft. (60 cm) tall. Oval midlength glossy green leaves in triplets on long stems. Subspecies and cultivars include *stewardsonii, triphyllum,* and 'zebrinum'.

Bloom: Spring–early summer. Brown, green, purple, with lighter veins. Solitary spiral spathe with narrow leaflike form protects clublike green, purple central spadix.

Plant hardiness: Zones 4–9. Ground hardy zones 5–9.

Soil: Well-drained. Fertility: Rich–average. 5.5–6.5 pH.

Planting: Autumn in partial shade to full shade. Space 10–12 in. (25–30 cm) apart, 3–4 in. (75–100 mm) deep.

Care: Moderate. Keep very moist spring–autumn. Fertilize monthly during growth. Mulch. Propagate by offsets, seed.

Storage: Dark, 50–60°F (10–16°C), in net bag or open basket of dry peat moss.

Features: Good choice for beds, borders, containers in indoor, woodland gardens. Deer, rodent resistant.

Bulb: Kangaroo-Paw. *Anigozanthos* species and hybrids. HAEMODORACEAE.

Description: Spring rhizome. Deciduous. About 10 species. Stands 18–48 in. (45–120 cm) tall. Straplike, midlength green leaves.

Bloom: Winter–spring. Green, orange, pink, red, yellow. Multiple narrow, cylinder-shaped flowers ¾–3 in. (20–75 mm) long atop long stalks.

Plant hardiness: Zones 8–11. Ground hardy zones 9–11.

Soil: Well-drained. Fertility: Rich. 6.0–6.5 pH.

Planting: Spring or early autumn in full sun. Space 2 ft. (60 cm) apart, at soil level.

Care: Moderate. Keep moist spring–autumn. Fertilize until buds form. Deadhead flowers. Remove withered foliage. Propagate by division in spring.

Storage: Dark, 50–60°F (10–16°C), in net bag or open basket of dry peat moss.

Features: Good choice for backgrounds, beds, borders, bouquets, containers in arid, cutting, rock gardens and greenhouses. Attracts bees, hummingbirds. Deer and snail, slug susceptible.

LILY

Nearly 100 species and thousands of hybrid members of the *Lilium* genus, all native to the northern temperate zone, are sensuous, sumptuous stars of cottage gardens and formal floral arrangements; their showy flowers can be found along mountain trails and country roadsides as well as in carefully maintained gardens. All are summer bloomers; most are true bulbs lacking tunicate sheaths with open scales.

While the North American Lily Society classifies lilies in nine divisions, most commonly planted are the following informal categories:

1. Asiatic Hybrid Lilies
2. Aurelian Hybrid Lilies
3. Oriental Hybrid Lilies
4. Species Lilies

Popular Asiatic hybrids bloom in early summer, their open flowers facing up, down, or outward. Aurelian hybrids stem from the Asiatic hybrids, but bloom in midsummer with fragrant, fluted or bowl-shaped flowers. Highly fragrant Oriental hybrids produce huge bowl-shaped blossoms to 10 in. (25 cm) wide in late summer or early autumn. Species lilies vary in habit, flower form, and bloom season. Colors run the gamut of copper, pinks, red, whites, and yellows, even bicolored, with bands, stripes, and speckles sometimes adding to their allure.

Lily flowers can be shaped like trumpets, shallow bowls, funnels, or cups, sometimes with as many as 20 or 30 blossoms on a stem. Many have petals that curve back gracefully to reveal large red, brown, or golden anthers loaded with pollen on long green filaments.

Plant most lilies in the autumn; in zones 9 and 10, place the bulbs in the vegetable keeper of a refrigerator for 4–6 weeks prior to planting unless they have been prechilled. The soil must be well-drained, deep, and loose. Supplement it with organic matter, if needed. Lilies thrive when their tops are in the sun while their roots are kept cool by the shade cast from shrubs or bushy perennials.

Plant them in borders or containers, or group them as garden accents. They also are excellent cut flowers. Deadhead spent blooms, leaving as much stem as possible—the foliage provides energy to developing offsets and the parent bulb.

Force lilies by chilling their bulbs, then planting in a deep pot filled with soil, covering the bulbs. Water, then place the container in a warm, well-lit location.

Bulb: Lily. *Lilium* species and hybrids. LILIACEAE.

Description: Summer bulb. Deciduous. About 100 species, many hybrids. Stands 2–6 ft. (60–180 cm) tall. Lance-shaped, midlength shiny, bright green leaves.

Bloom: Summer. Orange, purple, red, white, yellow, often speckled with contrasts. Solitary or multiple, trumpet- or star-shaped, often fragrant flowers 4–10 in. (10–25 cm) wide, usually with prominent stamens and often with reflexed petals.

Plant hardiness: Zones 3–10. Ground hardy zones 6–10.

Soil: Well-drained, moist. Fertility: Rich. 6.0–6.5 pH.

Planting: Autumn or early spring in full sun to partial shade. Space 6–12 in. (15–30 cm) apart, 6–12 in. (15–30 cm) deep, depending on species.

Care: Easy. Keep moist in summer; water plant at base. Fertilize during growth. Deadhead flowers. Mulch in summer. Propagate by offsets, bulbils in autumn.

Storage: Dark, 40–50°F (4–10°C), in net bag or open basket of dry peat moss.

Features: Good choice for accents, backgrounds, borders, bouquets, containers in cottage gardens and landscapes. Naturalizes. Deer, rodent susceptible and leaf fungus, lily-mosaic virus susceptible.

Bulb: Lily, Gloriosa; Climbing Lily. *Gloriosa superba*. LILIACEAE.
Description: Summer tuber. Deciduous. Stands to 8 ft. (2.4 m) tall.
Oval, pointed, short to midlength green leaves on climbing vine.
Bloom: Spring, summer, autumn. Orange, red, yellow, often edged in
green, red, yellow, white. Many shooting-star-like flowers 2–3 in.
(50–75 mm) long, often with frilly, fully reflexed petals.
Plant hardiness: Zones 7–11. Ground hardy zones 9–11.
Soil: Well-drained. Fertility: Rich. 6.0–6.5 pH.
Planting: Late spring–summer in full sun. Space 1–2 ft. (30–60 cm)
apart, 2 in. (50 mm) deep.
Care: Moderate. Keep moist spring–summer. Fertilize during growth.
Protect from wind. Stake to support. Propagate by division, offsets.
Storage: Dark, 60–70°F (16–21°C), in net bag or open basket of dry peat moss.
Features: Good choice for bouquets, containers, fences, lattices, trellises in cutting, tropical
gardens. Deer, rodent susceptible.

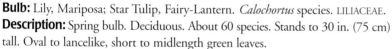

Bulb: Lily, Mariposa; Star Tulip, Fairy-Lantern. *Calochortus* species. LILIACEAE.
Description: Spring bulb. Deciduous. About 60 species. Stands to 30 in. (75 cm)
tall. Oval to lancelike, short to midlength green leaves.
Bloom: Spring–early summer. Pink, purple, red, white, yellow. Upright or
sometimes nodding, cup-shaped or globelike, sometimes hairy flowers 1–2 in.
(25–50 mm) long.
Plant hardiness: Zones 5–10. Ground hardy zones 5–8.
Soil: Well-drained sandy loam. Fertility: Average. 5.5–6.5 pH, varies by species.
Planting: Autumn in full sun to partial shade. Space 12–18 in. (30–45 cm) apart,
3–5 in. (75–125 mm) deep. In containers, space 1 in. (25 mm) apart, 2–3 in.
(50–75 mm) deep.
Care: Moderate. Keep moist spring–early summer. Fertilize first year in spring.
Deadhead blooms and flower stalks. Mulch. Lift in hot, moist-summer areas.
Propagate by offsets, seed.
Storage: Dark, 60°F (16°C), in net bag or open basket of dry peat moss or sand.
Features: Good choice for accents, bouquets, containers in cutting, rock gardens. Good for
bulb fanciers. Deer, rodent susceptible.

Bulb: Lily, Pineapple. *Eucomis* species. LILIACEAE.
Description: Summer bulb. Deciduous. About 15 species. Stands 12–30 in.
(30–75 cm) tall. Strap-shaped, midlength green leaves, sometimes speckled with
purple and often with ruffled edges.
Bloom: Summer. Greenish white, yellow, often edged in purple. Multiple star-
shaped, sometimes fragrant flowers ½–1¼ in. (12–30 mm) long, in snug tiers
along stalk, form pineapple-like foliage clusters above flowers.
Plant hardiness: Zones 6–11. Ground hardy zones 9–11.
Soil: Well-drained. Fertility: Rich. 6.0–6.5 pH.
Planting: Spring in partial shade. Space 6–8 in. (15–20 cm) apart, slightly below
soil level.
Care: Easy. Keep moist spring–autumn. Fertilize during growth. Mulch. Protect
from heat, zones 10–11. Propagate by offsets, seed. Divide when crowded.
Storage: Dark, 55–65°F (13–18°C), in net bag or open basket of dry peat moss.
Features: Good choice for beds, borders, bouquets, containers in cutting, shade,
woodland gardens. Deer, rodent susceptible.

Bulb: Lily, Torch; Red-Hot-Poker. *Kniphofia uvaria.* LILIACEAE.
Description: Summer rhizome. Deciduous or semi-evergreen, depending on climate. Stands to 4 ft. (1.2 m) tall. Broad, grasslike, long gray green leaves.
Bloom: Summer. Orange, red, turning yellow as blooms age. Many drooping, tube-shaped flowers 1 in. (25 mm) long, in tiers vertically atop fleshy stalk, form flamelike clusters 4–6 in. (10–15 cm) long.
Plant hardiness: Zones 5–10. Ground hardy zones 8–10.
Soil: Well-drained sandy loam. Fertility: Average–low. 5.5–6.5 pH.
Planting: Spring in full sun. Space 18 in. (45 cm) apart, barely covered.
Care: Moderate. Keep moist spring–early summer, dry late summer–autumn. Fertilize in spring. Mulch. Protect from frost, zones 5–7. Propagate by division, offsets, seed in early spring.
Storage: Dark, 40–50°F (4–10°C), in net bag or open basket of dry peat moss.
Features: Good choice for bouquets, mixed plantings in tropical gardens. Attracts hummingbirds. Evergreen in warm-winter climates.

Bulb: Lily-of-the-Incas; Peruvian Lily. *Alstroemeria* species. LILIACEAE.
Description: Summer rhizome or tuberous root. Deciduous. About 50 species. Stands 18–48 in. (45–120 cm) tall. Lancelike, short green leaves on stems.
Bloom: Late spring–summer. Purple, red, yellow, white, bicolored. Multiple flared, trumpet-shaped, often fragrant long-lasting flowers to 2 in. (50 mm) wide, in radiating clusters.
Plant hardiness: Zones 7–10. Ground hardy zones 8–10.
Soil: Well-drained. Fertility: Rich. 6.0–7.0 pH.
Planting: Spring in full sun to partial shade. Space 1 ft. (30 cm) apart, 6–8 in. (15–20 cm) deep.
Care: Moderate. Keep very moist during growth. Fertilize during growth. Mulch. Lift, zone 7. Propagate by division, seed in early spring or autumn. Use care: roots are brittle.
Storage: Dark, 50–60°F (10–16°C), in net bag or open basket of dry peat moss. Lift greenhouse container plants.
Features: Good choice for beds, borders, bouquets, containers in casual, cutting gardens. Avoid cutting; gently pull flower stems from rhizome. Naturalizes. Deer, rodent susceptible.

Bulb: Lily-of-the-Nile; Harriet's Flower. *Agapanthus* species. AMARYLLIDACEAE.
Description: Summer rhizome. Deciduous or evergreen, depending on species. Stands 18–48 in. (45–120 cm) tall. Swordlike, arching, midlength, thick, shiny, succulent green leaves.
Bloom: Summer. Blue, white. Multiple flared, tube-shaped flowers to 8 in. (20 cm) wide form dense, spherical clusters.
Plant hardiness: Zones 6–11. Ground hardy zones 7–11.
Soil: Well-drained. Fertility: Average. 5.5–6.5 pH.
Planting: Spring–autumn in full sun to partial shade. Space 1–2 ft. (30–60 cm) apart, slightly below soil level.
Care: Easy. Keep moist during growth. Fertilize during growth. Mulch in zones 6–8. Propagate by division in autumn, or seed in spring.
Storage: In-ground.
Features: Good choice for beds, borders, bouquets, containers, mass plantings in cottage, cutting, woodland gardens. Deer susceptible.

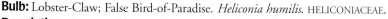

Bulb: Lily-of-the-Valley; Muget. *Convallaria majalis.* LILIACEAE.
Description: Spring rhizome. Deciduous. Stands to 8 in. (20 cm) tall. Broad, midlength light to dark green leaves, sometimes variegated.
Bloom: Spring. Pink, white. Multiple nodding, bell-shaped, fragrant flowers ¼–½ in. (6–12 mm) wide, in clusters of up to 20 per stem, form red berrylike fruits in autumn.
Plant hardiness: Zones 2–9. Ground hardy zones 2–7.
Soil: Well-drained to moist. Fertility: Rich–average. 5.5–6.5 pH.
Planting: Autumn or early spring in partial shade to full shade. Space 1–2 ft. (30–60 cm) apart, 1½–3 in. (38–75 mm) deep.
Care: Moderate. Keep moist year-round. Mulch. Propagate by division, pips; start pips 4–6 in. (10–15 cm) apart, transplant to garden in autumn.
Storage: Dark, 40–50°F (4–10°C), in porous container of dampened peat moss.
Features: Good choice for bouquets, containers, ground covers in cottage, cutting, woodland gardens. Naturalizes. Deer, rodent resistant. Mealybug susceptible.

Bulb: Lobster-Claw; False Bird-of-Paradise. *Heliconia humilis.* HELICONIACEAE.
Description: Summer rhizome. Evergreen. Stands to 4 ft. (1.2 m) tall. Spoonlike long, mid- to dark green leaves.
Bloom: Summer–autumn. Orange, red, yellow. Multiple lobster-claw-like flowers 5–10 in. (13–25 cm) long, in tiers vertically atop stalk.
Plant hardiness: Zones 10–11. Ground hardy zones 10–11.
Soil: Well-drained moist sandy loam. Fertility: Rich. 6.0–6.5 pH.
Planting: Spring–autumn in partial shade. Space 3 ft. (90 cm) apart, as deep as the soil level in the nursery container.
Care: Moderate. Keep moist spring–autumn. Fertilize monthly during growth. Protect from wind. Propagate by division.
Storage: In-ground. Maintain year-round.
Features: Good choice for accents, borders, bouquets, containers in tropical gardens and greenhouses.

Bulb: Lords-and-Ladies. *Arum italicum.* ARACEAE.
Description: Spring tuber. Deciduous. Stands 12–18 in. (30–45 cm) tall. Elongated heart-shaped green leaves with cream variegated patterns.
Bloom: Spring. Green, purple, white, yellow. Solitary, nearly spiral spathe with narrow leaflike form protects central spadix to 8 in. (20 cm) tall, which forms attractive orange, red berries. Resembles Jack-in-the-pulpit; both are members of ARACEAE family. A related species, *A. maculatum*, with black spotted foliage, is commonly cultivated.
Plant hardiness: Zones 5–10. Ground hardy zones 6–10, depending on species.
Soil: Well-drained. Fertility: Rich–average. 6.5–7.5 pH.
Planting: Autumn in partial shade to full shade. Space 1 ft. (30 cm) apart, 3–4 in. (75–100 mm) deep.
Care: Easy. Keep moist spring–summer. Fertilize in spring. Mulch. Protect from wind. Propagate by division in late summer–early autumn.
Storage: Dark, 50–60°F (10–16°C), in net bag or open basket of dry peat moss.
Features: Good choice for beds, borders, bouquets in cutting, indoor, woodland gardens. Deer, rodent resistant.

Warning

Berries of lords-and-ladies are hazardous if ingested. Avoid planting in areas frequented by children or pets.

Bulb: Meadow Saffron; Autumn Crocus. *Colchicum autumnale.* LILIACEAE.

Description: Autumn corm. Deciduous. Stands 4–12 in. (10–30 cm) tall. Straplike midlength green leaves in spring after flowers.

Bloom: Late summer–early autumn. Purple, white, yellow. Multiple flared, crocuslike flowers to 4 in. (10 cm) wide.

Plant hardiness: Zones 4–9. Ground hardy zones 7–9.

Soil: Well-drained. Fertility: Average. 5.5–6.5 pH.

Planting: Summer in full sun. Space 6–8 in. (15–20 cm) apart, 3–4 in. (75–100 mm) deep.

Care: Easy. Keep moist autumn–spring. Fertilize during growth. Mulch, zones 3–5. Propagate by division, cormels in summer. Divide only when crowded.

Storage: Dark, 40–50°F (4–10°C), in net bag or open basket of dry peat moss.

Features: Good choice for borders in woodland gardens. Naturalizes. Deer, rodent resistant.

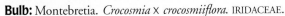

Bulb: Montebretia. *Crocosmia* x *crocosmiiflora.* IRIDACEAE.

Description: Summer corm. Deciduous. Many hybrids. Stands to 4 ft. (1.2 m) tall. Swordlike long green leaves.

Bloom: Summer. Orange, red, yellow. Multiple funnel-shaped flowers, 1½–2 in. (38–50 mm) wide, with widely flared petals, form tiers vertically along one side of multiple angled, branching spikes.

Plant hardiness: Zones 6–11. Ground hardy zones 8–10.

Soil: Well-drained, moist. Fertility: Average. 5.5–6.5 pH.

Planting: Spring in partial shade. Space 4–6 in. (10–15 cm) apart, 2–4 in. (50–100 mm) deep.

Care: Easy. Keep moist spring–autumn. Fertilize in spring. Mulch in zones 6–7. Propagate by division, offsets, seed.

Storage: Dark, 50–60°F (10–16°C), in net bag or open basket of dry peat moss.

Features: Good choice for beds, borders, containers, drifts, edgings, mixed plantings in cottage, meadow gardens and landscapes. Attracts hummingbirds. Naturalizes. Drought tolerant. Invasive zones 9–10.

Bulb: Morning-Glory, Bush; Man Root. *Ipomoea leptophylla.* CONVOLVULACEAE.

Description: Summer tuber. Deciduous. Stands to 4 ft. (1.2 m) tall. Very narrow, heart-shaped midlength green leaves.

Bloom: Summer. Pink, purple, white. Multiple round, flute- or cone-shaped flowers to 4 in. (10 cm) wide. Blooms only on new growth. Flowers close at night.

Plant hardiness: Zones 5–10. Ground hardy zones 5–10.

Soil: Well-drained sandy loam. Fertility: Average. 6.0–7.0 pH.

Planting: Early autumn in full sun for tubers; spring for seed. Space 5 ft. (1.5 m) apart, 2–4 in. (50–100 mm) deep for tubers; ¼ in. (6 mm) deep for seed. Scarify and soak seed before planting.

Care: Easy. Keep moist spring–summer. Fertilize during growth. Mulch, zones 9–10. Prune for compact growth. Propagate by cuttings, division, seed.

Storage: Dark, 50–60°F (10–16°C), in porous container of dampened peat moss.

Features: Good choice for accents, backgrounds, containers in arid, cottage, meadow gardens. Very drought tolerant. Develops very large tap root, to 2 ft. (60 cm) wide and 5 ft. (1.5 m) long.

Bulb: Naked Lily; Magic Lily; Spider Lily. *Lycoris* species. AMARYLLIDACEAE.

Description: Autumn bulb. Deciduous. About 11 species. Stands to 2 ft. (60 cm) tall. Narrow, straplike, midlength green leaves usually appear after bloom.

Bloom: Late summer–autumn. Pink, red, white, yellow. Flared, trumpetlike, sometimes fragrant flowers to 3 in. (75 mm) long with extended stamens.

Plant hardiness: Zones 4–11, depending on species or cultivar. Ground hardy zones 7–10.

Soil: Well-drained sandy loam. Fertility: Average. 6.0–7.0 pH.

Planting: Late summer in full sun. Space 6–8 in. (15–20 cm) apart, slightly below soil level.

Care: Moderate–challenging. Keep moist autumn–spring, dry in summer. Fertilize during growth. Propagate by offsets, seed. Best left undisturbed. Needs dry summer heat for reliable blooms.

Storage: Dark, 50–60°F (10–16°C), in net bag or open basket of dry peat moss.

Features: Good choice for borders, containers, mixed plantings in meadow, rock gardens. Plant with ornamental grasses, ferns to provide foliage backdrop. *L. radiata* naturalizes. Deer, rodent resistant.

Bulb: Nasturtium, Bitter Indian; Tuber Nasturtium. *Tropaeolum tuberosum.* TROPAEOLACEAE.

Description: Summer tuber. Deciduous. About 50 species. Stands to 15 ft. (4.5 m) tall. Rounded, deeply lobed, short green leaves.

Bloom: Spring–summer. Orange, purple, red, yellow, sometimes speckled, striped with contrasts. Nodding fuschialike flowers, to 1 in. (25 mm) long.

Plant hardiness: Zones 8–11. Ground hardy zones 9–11.

Soil: Well-drained sandy loam. Fertility: Average. 5.5–7.0 pH.

Planting: Autumn in full sun, zones 9–11; spring, zone 8. Space 3–5 ft. (90–150 cm) apart, 1–2 in. (25–50 cm) deep.

Care: Moderate. Keep moist during growth. Fertilize during growth. Propagate by division, seed.

Storage: Dark, 50–60°F (10–16°C), in net bag or open basket of dry peat moss.

Features: Good choice for fences, lattices, trellises, walls in cottage gardens and landscapes.

Bulb: Nerine; Guernsey Lily. *Nerine* species. AMARYLLIDACEAE.

Description: Autumn bulb. Deciduous or semi-evergreen. About 30 species. Stands to 3 ft. (90 cm) tall. Straplike, midlength deep green leaves.

Bloom: Autumn. Pink, red, white. Multiple wide-flared flowers, 2–3 in. (50–75 mm) wide, with curved petal tips, form ruffled clusters atop long stalks.

Plant hardiness: Zones 8–11. Ground hardy zones 8–11.

Soil: Well-drained sandy loam. Fertility: Average. 6.0–7.0 pH.

Planting: Late summer–autumn in full sun. Space 10–12 in. (25–30 cm) apart, slightly above soil level.

Care: Easy. Keep moist autumn–spring, allow deciduous varieties to dry in summer. Fertilize during growth. Mulch. Propagate by offsets. Best left undisturbed.

Storage: Dark, 50–60°F (10–16°C), in net bag or open basket of dry peat moss.

Features: Good choice for accents, backgrounds, beds, bouquets, containers in cottage, cutting, indoor, small-space gardens and greenhouses. Long-lasting flowers. Deer, rodent resistant.

ORNAMENTAL ONION

Between 400 and 500 species and numerous hybrids in the genus *Allium* are beautiful flowering bulbs comprising chive, garlic, leek, onion, and shallot. All are spring- or summer-bloomers, with bulbous or rhizomatous roots. They feature pom-pom-like or clustered flowers on long, hollow stalks in a variety of colors from blue and red to yellow.

In the landscape, they are eye catching for their unusual form. Use them for massed plantings, edgings, borders, and in container plantings in full sun to partial shade. They are hardy to very cold temperatures if mulched in the autumn.

Several species and cultivars provide choices for height, color, and appearance:

1. *A. aflatunense*
   pink flowers, 5 ft. (1.5 m)
2. *A. atropurpureum*
   purple flowers, 30 in. (75 cm)
3. Blue Allium (*A. caeruleum*)
   blue flowers, 1 ft. (30 cm)
4. *A. carinatum* var. *pulchellum*
   red purple flowers, 2 ft. (60 cm)
5. Nodding Onion (*A. cernuum*)
   pink flowers, 18 in. (45 cm)
6. Stars-of-Persia (*A. christophii*)
   blue flowers, 16 in. (40 cm)
7. *A. flavum*
   yellow flowers, 1 ft. (30 cm)
8. Giant Allium (*A. giganteum*)
   blue violet flowers, 4 ft. (1.2 m)
9. *A. karataviense*
   white flowers, 6 in. (15 cm)
10. *A. macleanii*
    Purple flowers, 4 ft. (1.2 m)
11. Golden Garlic (*A. moly*)
    yellow flowers, 18 in. (45 cm)
12. *A. narcissiflorum*
    deep pink flowers, 1 ft. (30 cm)
13. Daffodil Garlic (*A. neapolitanum*)
    white flowers, 1 ft. (30 cm)
14. *A. oreophilum*
    bright pink flowers, 6 in. (15 cm)
15. *A. rosenbachianum* 'Album'
    violet flowers, 1 ft. (30 cm)
16. *A. roseum*
    pink flowers, 10–24 in. (25–60 cm)
17. Chives (*A. sphaerocephalon*)
    purple flowers, 3 ft. (90 cm)
18. *A. triquetrum*
    white, green flowers, 18 in. (45 cm)
19. Garlic Chive (*A. tuberosum*)
    white flowers, 1 ft. (30 cm)
20. *A. unifolium*
    pink flowers, 16 in. (40 cm)

Bulb: Onion, Ornamental; Allium. *Allium* species. LILIACEAE.

Description: Summer bulb. Deciduous. About 700 species. Stands 6–60 in. (15–150 cm) tall. Narrow or broad, usually hollow, midlength gray green leaves.

Bloom: Spring–summer. Blue, pink, red, violet, white, yellow. Multiple star-shaped, often fragrant flowers ¼–1 in. (6–25 mm) wide form compact or loose clusters 1–6 in. (25–150 mm) wide on tall, leafless stems, bearing seed and bulbils.

Plant hardiness: Zones 3–10. Ground hardy zones 4–8.

Soil: Well-drained humus. Fertility: Average. 6.0–7.0 pH.

Planting: Autumn in full sun to partial shade. Space 4–12 in. (10–30 cm) apart, 2–8 in. (50–200 mm) deep, depending on species.

Care: Easy. Keep moist winter–spring. Fertilize in spring. Deadhead flowers. Mulch, zones 3–5. Propagate by division, offsets, bulbils in autumn, seed in spring.

Storage: Dark, 50–60°F (10–16°C), in net bag or open basket of dry peat moss.

Features: Good choice for accents, borders, containers, drying, edgings in cottage, formal, meadow, natural, rock, woodland gardens. Naturalizes. Pest and disease, deer and rodent resistant.

Bulb: Orchid Pansy; Nut Orchid; Mother's-Tears. *Achimenes* species. GESNERIACEAE.
Description: Summer rhizome. Deciduous. About 26 species. Stands 1–2 ft. (30–60 cm) tall, often trailing. Oval, toothed, short, textured, hairy olive green leaves, often with burgundy undersides.
Bloom: Summer–autumn. Blue, orange, pink, purple, red, yellow, white. Multiple flutelike flowers 1–2 in. (25–50 mm) long with thin or broad, flared petals.
Plant hardiness: Zones 4–11. Ground hardy zones 9–11.
Soil: Well-drained humus. Fertility: Rich. 6.0–7.5 pH.
Planting: Late spring–early summer in partial shade. Protect from summer heat. Space 6–10 in. (15–25 cm) apart, 1 in. (25 mm) deep. In containers, space 1–2 in. (25–50 mm) apart.
Care: Easy. Keep moist spring–summer. Fertilize during growth; dilute fertilizer to half the recommended rate. Mulch. Stake or allow to trail. Propagate by division.
Storage: Dark, 50–60°F (10–16°C), in porous container of dampened peat moss.
Features: Good choice for hanging baskets, beds, borders, containers, edgings in container, hanging gardens. Deer, rodent resistant. Spider mite, thrip susceptible.

Bulb: Peacock Orchid; Fragrant Gladiolus; Abyssinian Sword Lily. *Gladiolus callianthus (Acidanthera bicolor).* IRIDACEAE.
Description: Autumn corm. Deciduous. Stands 2–3 ft. (60–90 cm) tall. Narrow, straplike, long midgreen leaves.
Bloom: Late summer–early autumn. White, with brown contrasts. Multiple orchidlike, fragrant flowers to 3 in. (75 mm) wide atop long stems.
Plant hardiness: Zones 6–11. Ground hardy zones 9–11.
Soil: Well-drained. Fertility: Average. 6.5–7.0 pH.
Planting: Spring in partial shade. Space 6–8 in. (15–20 cm) apart, 4–6 in. (10–15 cm) deep.
Care: Moderate. Keep moist spring–autumn. Fertilize monthly during growth. Mulch. Propagate by cormels.
Storage: Dark, 50–60°F (10–16°C), in net bag or open basket of dry peat moss.
Features: Good choice for accents, beds, borders, containers, cutting, edgings in arid, hanging, rock, tropical gardens.

Bulb: Persian Buttercup; Florist's Ranunculus. *Ranunculus asiaticus* and hybrids. RANUNCULACEAE.
Description: Spring tuberous root. Deciduous. Stands 18 in. (45 cm) tall. Fernlike, midlength, deeply toothed, dark green leaves, thinly spaced.
Bloom: Early spring–summer, depending on zone. Orange, pink, purple, red, white, yellow. Multiple round, single or tightly layered, camellia-like flowers 1½ in. (38 mm) wide atop long stems.
Plant hardiness: Zones 4–11. Ground hardy zones 8–9.
Soil: Well-drained sandy loam. Fertility: Average–low. 5.5–6.0 pH.
Planting: Autumn in full to partial sun, zones 8–11; spring, zones 4–7. Space 4–6 in. (10–15 cm) apart, 1–2 in. (25–50 mm) deep. Soak for 24 hours before you plant.
Care: Easy. Keep moist autumn–early spring. Keep damp late spring–summer. Fertilize in spring. Mulch, zones 4–8. Propagate by division.
Storage: Dark, 50–60°F (10–16°C), in net bag or open basket of dry peat moss.
Features: Good choice for beds, borders, bouquets, containers, drifts in cottage, cutting, rock gardens. Deer, rodent resistant. Snail, slug susceptible.

Bulb: Scarborough Lily. *Cyrtanthus elatus (C. purpurea, Vallota speciosa).*
AMARYLLIDACEAE.
Description: Spring, summer, or autumn bulb. Evergreen. Stands 3 ft. (90 cm) tall.
Straplike, long green leaves.
Bloom: Summer–autumn. Scarlet, sometimes pink, white. Multiple flared, six-
petaled, trumpet-shaped, often fragrant flowers 3–4 in. (75–100 mm) wide.
Plant hardiness: Zones 9–11. Ground hardy zones 9–11.
Soil: Well-drained. Fertility: Rich. 6.0–6.8 pH.
Planting: Spring in full sun. Space 6–12 in. (15–30 cm) apart, at soil level. In
6-in. (15-cm) container, plant single bulb with top one-third above soil.
Care: Moderate. Keep moist through bloom, dry when dormant. Fertilize until
buds form. Protect from heat. Propagate by offsets in summer. Divide only
when crowded.
Storage: Dark, 55–65°F (13–18°C), in net bag or open basket of dry peat moss.
Features: Good choice for accents, beds, containers in indoor, cottage, patio, small-
space, woodland gardens. Good houseplant.

Bulb: Snowdrop. *Galanthus* species. AMARYLLIDACEAE.
Description: Spring bulb. Deciduous. More than 15 species. Stands 6–12 in.
(15–30 cm) tall. Narrow, short to midlength bright green leaves in groups of 2 or 3.
Bloom: Late winter–early spring. White. Solitary, nodding, drop-shaped flowers
1–2 in. (25–50 mm) wide.
Plant hardiness: Zones 2–10. Ground hardy zones 4–7.
Soil: Well-drained humus. Fertility: Rich–average. 6.0–6.5 pH.
Planting: Autumn in partial shade. Space 4–6 in. (10–15 cm) apart, 3–4 in.
(75–100 mm) deep.
Care: Easy. Keep moist autumn–spring. Fertilize in spring. Mulch. Propagate by
division when dormant.
Storage: Dark, 40–50°F (4–10°C), in net bag or open basket of dry peat moss.
Features: Good choice for beds, borders, containers, edgings, mixed plantings, turf
in meadow, rock, woodland gardens. Naturalizes. Deer, rodent resistant.

Bulb: Snowflake. *Leucojum* species. AMARYLLIDACEAE.
Description: Spring, summer, or autumn bulb. Deciduous. About nine
species. Stands 8–16 in. (20–40 cm) tall. Straplike, midlength, thin dark
green leaves.
Bloom: Spring, autumn, depending on species. White, with green,
red, yellow tints. Dainty, nodding, bell-shaped flowers ½–1 in.
(12–25 mm) long with spring green highlights.
Plant hardiness: Zones 3–11. Ground hardiness varies by species.
Soil: Well-drained to moist, depending on species. Fertility: Average.
6.0–6.5 pH.
Planting: Autumn in full to filtered sun. Follow grower directions for
each species. Space 4 in. (10 cm) apart, 4 in. (10 cm) deep.
Care: Easy. Keep moist autumn–late spring, dry in summer. Fertilize annually in spring.
Mulch. Propagate by bulblets, division. Best left undisturbed.
Storage: Dark, 40–60°F (4–16°C), in net bag or open basket of dry peat moss.
Features: Good choice for beds, borders, bouquets in cutting, meadow, natural, woodland
gardens, water margins. Naturalizes. Deer, rodent resistant. *L. aestivum* blooms in spring,
L. autumnale in summer–autumn, *L. vernum* in late winter–early spring.

Bulb: Society Garlic. *Tulbaghia violacea.* AMARYLLIDACEAE.

Description: Summer bulb. Evergreen. Stands to 30 in. (75 cm) tall. Swordlike, midlength, thin gray green leaves. Cultivars include 'Silver Lace,' 'Tricolor', and 'variegata' with colorful leaf variegations.

Bloom: Late spring–summer. Lavender, white. Multiple flared, tube-shaped, starlike fragrant flowers ¾–1 in. (20–25 mm) long in clusters atop tall, narrow stems.

Plant hardiness: Zones 8–11. Ground hardy zones 9–11.

Soil: Well-drained sandy loam. Fertility: Average. 6.5–7.5 pH.

Planting: Spring in full sun. Space 12–18 in. (30–45 cm) apart, 2 in. (50 mm) deep.

Care: Easy. Keep moist spring–autumn. Allow soil to dry between waterings. Fertilize during growth; dilute fertilizer to half the package-recommended rate. Mulch. Protect from frost, zones 8–9. Propagate by division, offsets, seed. Divide only when crowded.

Storage: Dark, 50–60°F (10–16°C), in net bag or open basket of dry peat moss.

Features: Good choice for accents, beds, borders, bouquets, containers in cutting, meadow gardens and landscapes. Drought tolerant when established. Deer, rodent resistant.

Bulb: Southern Swamp Lily. *Crinum americanum.* LILIACEAE.

Description: Spring bulb. Deciduous. Stands to 4 ft. (1.2 m) tall. Swordlike, arching, long green leaves.

Bloom: Spring–summer. Pink, white. Multiple flared, trumpet-shaped, fragrant flowers 4–5 in. (10–13 cm) long atop tall stalks.

Plant hardiness: Zones 7–11. Ground hardy zones 8–11.

Soil: Moist or water margins, to 6 in. (15 cm) deep. Fertility: Rich–average. 5.5–6.5 pH.

Planting: Autumn in full sun, zones 9–11; spring, zones 7–8. Space 18 in. (45 cm) apart, neck slightly above soil level.

Care: Easy. Keep very moist. Fertilize during growth. Mulch, zones 8–9. Protect from frost. Propagate by offsets, seed.

Storage: Dark, 50–60°F (10–16°C), in porous container of dampened peat moss.

Features: Good choice for accents, beds, borders, containers in meadow, water, woodland gardens. Deer, rodent resistant.

Bulb: Spider Lily; Crown-Beauty, Sea Daffodil. *Hymenocallis* species. AMARYLLIDACEAE.

Description: Summer bulb. Deciduous. More than 30 species. Stands 10–36 in. (25–90 cm) tall. Mostly straplike, long green leaves.

Bloom: Summer. Ivory, white. Graceful, morning-glory-like, fragrant flowers to 6 in. (15 cm) wide with long, thin petal tendrils.

Plant hardiness: Zones 6–10. Ground hardy zones 8–10.

Soil: Well-drained sandy loam. Fertility: Rich–average. 6.0–6.5 pH.

Planting: Spring in full sun. Space 6–18 in. (15–45 cm) apart, depending on species, slightly above soil level.

Care: Easy. Keep moist spring–summer. Fertilize during growth. Mulch, zones 6–8. Protect from wind. Propagate by division, offsets, seed.

Storage: Dark, 60–70°F (16–21°C), in net bag or open basket of dry peat moss.

Features: Good choice for beds, borders, bouquets, containers in indoor, tropical, water gardens. Deer, rodent resistant.

Bulb: Squill. *Scilla* species. LILIACEAE.

Description: Spring bulb. Deciduous. About 90 species. Stands 4–18 in. (10–45 cm) tall. Straplike, short to long green leaves.

Bloom: Early spring. Blue, pink, purple, white. Multiple star-shaped flowers to 1 in. (25 mm) wide form tiers along a single stalk or tight clusters atop foliage, depending on species.

Plant hardiness: Zones 3–11. Ground hardy zones 4–8, depending on species.

Soil: Well-drained humus. Fertility: Rich. 6.0–7.0 pH.

Planting: Autumn in full sun to partial shade, depending on species. Space 4–6 in. (10–15 cm) apart, 4 in. (10 cm) deep.

Care: Easy. Keep moist autumn–summer. Fertilize monthly during growth. Mulch. Propagate by offsets, seed.

Storage: Dark, 40–50°F (4–10°C), in net bag or open basket of dry peat moss.

Features: Good choice for borders, bouquets, containers, edgings, mass plantings, paths in cutting, formal, small-space, woodland gardens. Naturalizes.

Bulb: Star Grass. *Hypoxis* species. HYPOXIDACEAE.

Description: Spring cormlike rhizome. Evergreen. About 150 species. Stands to 1 ft. (30 cm) tall. Narrow, grasslike, midlength green leaves.

Bloom: Spring–summer. White, yellow. Solitary or multiple star-shaped flowers to 1 in. (25 mm) wide float amid narrow, chivelike leaves.

Plant hardiness: Zones 4–10. Ground hardy zones 6–10, depending on species.

Soil: Well-drained. Fertility: Average. 4.0–5.0 pH.

Planting: Autumn in full sun, spring for transplants. Space 6–8 in. (15–20 cm) apart, 4 in. (10 cm) deep.

Care: Moderate–challenging. Keep damp; allow soil to dry between waterings. Fertilize occasionally during growth; dilute fertilizer to half the recommended rate. Propagate by division, offsets, seed.

Storage: Dark, 40–50°F (4–10°C), in net bag or open basket of dry peat moss.

Features: Good choice for beds, containers, edgings, mixed plantings in meadow, natural, woodland gardens. Drought tolerant.

Bulb: Star-of-Bethlehem; Chincherinchee. *Ornithogalum* species. LILIACEAE.

Description: Spring or summer bulb, depending on species. Deciduous. About 80 species. Stands 1–3 ft. (30–90 cm) tall. Straplike, arching, glossy green leaves.

Bloom: Spring or summer. Orange, green white, white, yellow. Multiple six-petaled, star-shaped, often fragrant flowers 2–5 in. (50–125 mm) wide in tiers ascending vertically atop stalks.

Plant hardiness: Zones 4–10. Ground hardy zones 4–10, depending on species.

Soil: Well-drained. Fertility: Rich. 6.0–7.0 pH.

Planting: Autumn in full sun to partial shade. Space 6–8 in. (15–20 cm) apart, 3–5 in. (75–125 mm) deep.

Care: Easy. Keep moist autumn–spring. Fertilize during growth. Mulch, zones 4–8. Propagate by offsets, seed.

Storage: Dark, 50–60°F (10–16°C), in net bag or open basket of dry peat moss.

Features: Good choice for beds, borders, bouquets, containers in cutting, natural, woodland gardens. Naturalizes. Deer, rodent resistant.

Warning

The bulb and foliage of star-of-Bethlehem are hazardous if ingested. Avoid planting in gardens frequented by children and pets.

Bulb: Starflower, Spring. *Ipheion uniflorum (Brodiaea uniflora, Triteleia uniflora).* LILIACEAE.

Description: Spring bulb. Deciduous. Stands 6–8 in. (15–20 cm) tall. Flat, straplike, midlength, thin green leaves, with onionlike scent. Cultivars include 'Album', 'Rolf Fiedler', 'Violaceum', and 'Wisley Blue' with bloom size and color variations.

Bloom: Early spring. Blue, white. Simple star-shaped, often fragrant flowers to 1½ in. (38 mm) wide.

Plant hardiness: Zones 6–10. Ground hardy zones 6–9.

Soil: Well-drained. Fertility: Average. 6.0–7.0 pH.

Planting: Autumn in full sun to partial shade. Space 2–4 in. (50–100 mm) apart, 2 in. (50 mm) deep.

Care: Easy. Keep moist autumn–spring. Fertilize during growth until established. Propagate by division, offsets. Divide when crowded.

Storage: Dark, 40–50°F (4–10°C), in net bag or open basket of dry peat moss.

Features: Good choice for borders, containers, drifts, edgings, mass plantings in meadows, natural, rock, woodland gardens. Naturalizes. Deer, rodent resistant.

Bulb: Striped Squill. *Puschkinia scilloides.* LILIACEAE.

Description: Spring bulb. Deciduous. Stands to 6 in. (15 cm) tall. Straplike, midlength, thin dark green leaves.

Bloom: Late winter–spring. Blue white, white. Multiple nodding, partly flared, starlike flowers ½ in. (12 mm) long, in dense clusters atop stalk.

Plant hardiness: Zones 3–10. Ground hardy zones 4–8.

Soil: Well-drained sandy loam. Fertility: Average. 6.0–7.5 pH.

Planting: Autumn in partial shade. Space 2–3 in. (50–75 mm) apart, 2–4 in. (50–100 mm) deep.

Care: Easy. Keep moist in spring, dry after bloom. Fertilize in spring. Mulch. Protect from heat. Propagate by offsets when dormant.

Storage: Dark, 40–50°F (4–10°C), in net bag or open basket of dry peat moss.

Features: Good choice for borders, containers, drifts, edgings in meadows, natural, woodland gardens and landscapes. Naturalizes. Deer, rodent resistant.

Bulb: Summer Hyacinth. *Galtonia candicans.* LILIACEAE.

Description: Summer bulb. Deciduous. Stands 2–4 ft. (60–120 cm) tall. Straplike long green leaves.

Bloom: Late summer–autumn. Green white, white. Nodding, bell-shaped, fragrant flowers to 1½ in. (38 cm) long in tiers ascending vertically on tall stalk.

Plant hardiness: Zones 6–10. Ground hardy zones 8–10.

Soil: Well-drained humus. Fertility: Rich–average. 5.5–6.5 pH.

Planting: Autumn in full sun to partial shade, zones 9–10; spring, zones 6–8. Space 8–12 in. (20–30 cm) apart, 6 in. (15 cm) deep.

Care: Easy–moderate. Keep moist in spring, dry in summer. Fertilize during growth. Mulch, zones 6–8. Propagate by offsets, seed.

Storage: Dark, 50–60°F (10–16°C), in net bag or open basket of dry peat moss.

Features: Good choice for backgrounds, beds, borders, bouquets, containers in cottage, cutting, natural, woodland gardens and landscapes. Deer, rodent resistant. Slug, snail susceptible.

Bulb: Tiger Flower; Mexican Shell Flower. *Tigridia pavonia.* IRIDACEAE.
Description: Summer corm. Deciduous. Stands to 3 ft. (90 cm) tall. Swordlike, vertically ribbed, long thin green leaves.
Bloom: Summer–autumn. Orange, pink, purple, red, white, yellow. Cuplike or open tripetaled, nearly triangular flowers to 3 in. (75 mm) wide, with inset, curved, inner petals and speckled, contrasting-colored centers. Succession of blooms, each lasting a single day.
Plant hardiness: Zones 4–11. Ground hardy zones 7–9.
Soil: Well-drained. Fertility: Average. 6.0–7.0 pH.
Planting: Late spring in full sun. Space 4–6 in. (10–15 cm) apart, 2–3 in. (50–75 mm) deep.
Care: Moderate. Keep moist spring–summer. Fertilize during growth. Mulch, zones 4–8. Lift, zones 4–6. Protect from heat, frost. Propagate by cormlets, offsets, seed.
Storage: Dark, 50–60°F (10–16°C), in net bag or open basket of dry peat moss.
Features: Good choice for beds, borders, containers, mixed plantings in tropical gardens and landscapes. Deer, rodent, and spider mite susceptible.

Bulb: Tree Gloxinia; Isoloma. *Kohleria* hybrids. GESNERIACEAE.
Description: Summer rhizome. Deciduous. Stands 1–3 ft. (30–90 cm) tall. Oval, finely toothed, short, velvety, dark gray green leaves, often with brown, purple, red undersides, and sometimes in a whorled pattern.
Bloom: Summer. Pink, red, yellow, often bicolored. Nodding, flared, tube-shaped flowers 1–2 in. (25–50 mm) long with round, bulbous petals.
Plant hardiness: Zones 8–11. Ground hardy zones 10–11.
Soil: Well-drained sandy loam. Fertility: Rich. 6.0–7.0 pH.
Planting: Spring in partial shade. Space 8–12 in. (20–30 cm) apart, 1–2 in. (25–50 mm) deep.
Care: Moderate. Keep moist spring–autumn. Fertilize monthly during growth. Mulch. Propagate by cuttings, division, seed. Prefers humid climates.
Storage: Dark, 50–60°F (10–16°C), in net bag or open basket of dry peat moss.
Features: Good choice for accents, beds, borders, containers in tropical gardens, landscapes, and greenhouses.

Bulb: Tuberose. *Polianthes tuberosa.* AGAVACEAE.
Description: Summer rhizome. Deciduous. Stands to 42 in. (1.1 m) tall. Narrow, grasslike, long green leaves.
Bloom: Summer–autumn. White. Multiple wide-flared single or double tube-shaped, very fragrant flowers in tiers ascending and surrounding top of stalk.
Plant hardiness: Zones 8–11. Ground hardy zones 9–11.
Soil: Well-drained humus. Fertility: Rich. **6.0–6.5** pH.
Planting: Spring in full sun. Space 6–8 in. (15–20 cm) apart, 2–3 in. (50–75 mm) deep. Best planted annually as new stock in cold-winter climates.
Care: Moderate–challenging. Keep moist spring–midautumn. Fertilize monthly during growth with acidic fertilizer. Propagate by division, offsets, seed.
Storage: Dark, 50–60°F (10–16°C), in net bag or open basket of dry peat moss.
Features: Good choice for beds, borders, bouquets, mixed plantings in cottage, cutting, meadow, small-space gardens. Naturalizes. Fragrance used in perfumes. Deer, rodent resistant. Aphid susceptible.

TULIP

Members of the diverse *Tulipa* genus are the most popular of all spring bulbs, and more than 100,000 hybrid cultivars have been registered. Most are native to southern Europe and the Mideast, though species tulips also are found in Asia's temperate zones.

Most tulips offered for home gardens are either hybrids or one of the 15 or so common species tulips suitable for naturalizing in lawn, turf, or beneath a leafy bower of deciduous trees. All species and hybrid tulips comprise groupings and divisions based on their flower type; for classification purposes, they first are grouped as botanical (species) or hybrid cultivars, then classified into one of 15 major divisions by the Royal Bulb Growers' Association, Netherlands:

Early Tulips—9–16 in. (23–40 cm):
  I. Single Early Tulips   II. Double Early Tulips
Mid-Season Tulips—16–26 in. (40–66 cm):
  III. Triumph Tulips   IV. Darwin Hybrid Tulips
Late-Season Tulips—16–36 in. (40–90 cm):
  V. Single Late Tulips (Darwin and Cottage)
  VI. Lily-Flowered Tulips   VII. Fringed Tulips
  VIII. Veridiflora Tulips   IX. Rembrandt Tulips
  X. Parrot Tulips   XI. Double Late Tulips (Peony-Flowered)
Species Tulips—size varies:
  XII. Kaufmanniana Tulips   XIII. Fosterana Tulips
  XIV. Greigii Tulips   XV. Other Species Tulips

Tulips grow in every color and hue except a true blue, have simple or exceedingly complex flowers, may have fringes or scalloped petals, and can serve many different garden and cut flower purposes. They look best when grouped together in massed plantings or used as a border in the landscape.

Bulb: Tulip. *Tulipa* species. LILIACEAE.
Description: Spring bulb. Deciduous. Up to 100 species, many hybrids and cultivars. Stands 5–24 in. (13–60 cm) tall. Broad to straplike, light to dark green leaves, sometimes patterned with stripes or mottled.
Bloom: Spring. All colors except blue; bi- and multicolored. Solitary single or double egg-shaped, sometimes fragrant flowers to 4 in. (10 cm) wide with rounded or pointed, smooth or fringed petals.
Plant hardiness: Zones 4–10. Ground hardy zones 4–7.
Soil: Well-drained. Fertility: Rich–average. 5.5–6.5 pH.
Planting: Autumn–winter in full sun to partial shade. Space 2–4 in. (50–100 mm) apart, 5–8 in. (13–20 cm) deep, depending on species.
Care: Easy. Keep moist winter–spring. Fertilize bimonthly in spring. Mulch, zones 8–10. Protect from wind. Propagate by offsets in late summer–autumn. Divide only when crowded. Transplant container plants to garden in second year.
Storage: Dark, 40–50°F (4–10°C), in net bag or open basket of dry peat moss.
Features: Good choice for accents, beds, borders, bouquets, containers, mass plantings in cottage, cutting, formal, woodland gardens. Most species tulips and some hybrids naturalize. Deer, rodent, and aphid susceptible.

Bulb: Wake-Robin; Trillium. *Trillium* species. LILIACEAE.

Description: Spring rhizome. Deciduous. About 30 species. Stands 6–20 in. (15–50 cm) tall. Oval, short to midlength green leaves in whorled groups of three.

Bloom: Spring. Purple, white, yellow. Solitary flowers 2–3 in. (50–75 mm) wide, usually with three, sharp-pointed petals.

Plant hardiness: Zones 2–9. Ground hardy zones 4–8.

Soil: Well-drained humus. Fertility: Rich. 6.0–7.0 pH.

Planting: Autumn in partial shade to full shade. Space 6–12 in. (15–30 cm) apart, 4 in. (10 cm) deep.

Care: Moderate. Keep moist year-round. Fertilize annually in spring. Mulch. Propagate by division, seed.

Storage: Dark, 40–50°F (4–10°C), in porous container of dampened peat moss.

Features: Good choice for accents, borders, drifts, edgings, mounds in natural, rock, shade, woodland gardens. Deer, rodent susceptible.

Bulb: Wandflower; Harlequin Flower. *Sparaxis* species. IRIDACEAE.

Description: Summer corm. Deciduous. About 6 species. Stands to 2 ft. (60 cm) tall. Narrow, swordlike, arching, light green leaves.

Bloom: Spring–early summer. Orange, pink, purple, red, white, yellow, bicolored. Multiple cup- to star-shaped flowers to 2 in. (50 mm) wide with flared petals and contrasting centers.

Plant hardiness: Zones 4–10. Ground hardy zones 7–10.

Soil: Well-drained sandy loam. Fertility: Average. 6.0–7.0 pH.

Planting: Autumn in full sun, zones 8–10; spring, zones 4–7. Space 3–4 in. (75–100 mm) apart, 2–4 in. (50–100 mm) deep. Best planted annually as new stock, zones 5–7.

Care: Easy. Keep moist autumn–spring. Fertilize monthly during growth. Mulch, zones 4–7. Propagate by cormels, offsets, seed.

Storage: Dark, 50–60°F (10–16°C), in net bag or open basket of dry peat moss.

Features: Good choice for accents, beds, borders, bouquets, containers, edgings, foregrounds, mixed plantings in cutting gardens and landscapes. Naturalizes. Deer, rodent susceptible.

Bulb: Windflower; Lily-of-the-Field. *Anemone* species. RANUNCULACEAE.

Description: Spring corm or rhizome. Deciduous. About 120 species. Stands 2–36 in. (5–90 cm) tall. Feathery, deeply toothed, small green leaves.

Bloom: Late winter–spring. Blue, pink, purple, red, white. Solitary daisy- or poppylike flowers to 3 in. (75 mm) wide with distinct centers and fleshy stems.

Plant hardiness: Zones 3–10, depending on species. Ground hardy zones 6–8.

Soil: Well-drained humus. Fertility: Rich. 6.0–7.5 pH, depending on species.

Planting: Autumn in full sun to partial shade, zones 8–10; spring, zones 3–7. Space 4–12 in. (10–30 cm) apart, 1–2 in. (25–50 mm) deep.

Care: Easy. Keep moist autumn–spring, dry in summer. Fertilize monthly during growth. Mulch, zones 3–6. Propagate by division, seed.

Storage: Rhizomes: dark, 40–50°F (4–10°C), in porous container of dampened peat moss; tubers: dark, 50–70°F (10–21°C), in open basket of dry peat moss.

Features: Good choice for beds, bouquets, containers, edgings, mixed plantings in meadow, natural, woodland gardens. Deer, rodent susceptible.

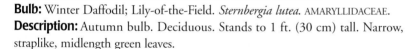

Bulb: Winter Aconite. *Eranthis hyemalis.* RANUNCULACEAE.
Description: Spring tuber. Deciduous. Stands 2–6 in. (50–150 mm) tall. Radiating, saucerlike, short bright green leaves. A related species, *E. cilicica*, bears reddish-tinged new foliage and larger blooms.
Bloom: Late winter–spring. Yellow. Cheerful, bright, cuplike, waxy flowers 1–1½ in. (25–38 mm) wide with collarlike foliage beneath.
Plant hardiness: Zones 3–8. Ground hardy zones 5–8.
Soil: Well-drained humus. Fertility: Rich–average. 6.0–6.5 pH.
Planting: Early autumn in full sun to partial shade. Space 2½–3 in. (63–75 mm) apart, 2 in. (50 mm) deep.
Care: Easy. Keep moist year-round; reduce watering after bloom. Fertilize in winter when growth first appears. Mulch. Protect from heat. Propagate by division, seed.
Storage: Dark, 40–50°F (4–10°C), in porous container of dampened peat moss.
Features: Good choice for borders, containers, edgings, mixed plantings in natural, rock, shade, woodland gardens and landscapes. Naturalizes. Deer, rodent resistant.

Bulb: Winter Daffodil; Lily-of-the-Field. *Sternbergia lutea.* AMARYLLIDACEAE.
Description: Autumn bulb. Deciduous. Stands to 1 ft. (30 cm) tall. Narrow, straplike, midlength green leaves.
Bloom: Autumn. Bright yellow. Solitary, freesialike, glossy flowers 1½ in. (38 mm) long form berrylike seeds.
Plant hardiness: Zones 6–9. Ground hardy zones 7–9.
Soil: Well-drained. Fertility: Rich–average. 6.5–7.5 pH.
Planting: Late summer in full sun. Space 4–6 in. (10–15 cm) apart, 4–6 in. (10–15 cm) deep.
Care: Easy. Keep moist autumn–spring, dry in summer. Fertilize during growth. Mulch, zones 6–7. Propagate by division, offsets, seed.
Storage: Dark, 40–50°F (4–10°C), in net bag or open basket of dry peat moss.
Features: Good choice for accents, beds, borders, containers, edgings in meadow, natural, rock gardens. Deer, rodent resistant. Spider mite susceptible.

Bulb: Wood Hyacinth; English and Spanish Bluebell. *Hyacinthoides* species (*Endymion* species, *Scilla* species). LILIACEAE.
Description: Spring bulb. Deciduous. About 4 species. Stands 20 in. (50 cm) tall. Narrow, arching, long green leaves.
Bloom: Spring. Blue, rose, pink, white. Multiple bell-shaped, fragrant flowers ¾ in. (20 mm) long in tiers vertically along a single stalk.
Plant hardiness: Zones 4–9. Ground hardy zones 5–9.
Soil: Well-drained to moist. Fertility: Rich. 6.0–7.0 pH.
Planting: Autumn in full sun to partial shade. Space 4–6 in. (10–15 cm) apart, 3–5 in. (75–125 mm) deep.
Care: Moderate. Keep moist winter–spring, damp in summer. Fertilize until buds form. Mulch, zones 4–6. Propagate by offsets, division. Divide only when crowded.
Storage: Dark, 40–50°F (4–10°C), in net bag or open basket of dry peat moss.
Features: Good choice for bouquets, drifts, mixed plantings in cottage, cutting, woodland gardens. Naturalizes. Deer, rodent resistant.

Bulb: Wood Sorrel. *Oxalis* species. OXALIDACEAE.
Description: Spring bulb, tuber, or rhizome, depending on species. Deciduous. More than 800 species. Stands 4–20 in. (10–50 cm) tall. Tufted, compact, or spreading. Cloverlike, small green, red, or gray green leaves, closing at night.
Bloom: Winter–summer. Pink, rose, white, yellow, often with contrasts at center. Solitary or multiple open or funnel-shaped flowers to 1 in. (25 mm) wide.
Plant hardiness: Zones 6–9. Ground hardy zones 7–9.
Soil: Well-drained. Fertility: Rich–average. 6.5–7.5 pH.
Planting: Late summer–autumn in full sun to partial shade. Space 2 in. (50 mm) apart, 1–4 in. (25–100 mm) deep.
Care: Easy. Keep moist spring–summer. Fertilize only at planting. Mulch, zones 6–8. Propagate by division, offsets, seed in autumn.
Storage: Dark, 50–60°F (10–16°C), in net bag or open basket of dry peat moss.
Features: Good choice for containers, ground cover in indoor, small-space, woodland gardens. Deer, rodent resistant. Tuberous and rhizomatous species are very invasive; plant in containers. Use only bulb species in garden soil plantings.

Bulb: Woodlily; Bush Lily. *Clivia* species. AMARYLLIDACEAE.
Description: Spring tuberous root. Evergreen. About four species. Stands to 2 ft. (60 cm) tall. Arching, straplike, long deep green leaves.
Bloom: Late winter–spring. Mostly orange with yellow centers, sometimes dark red, yellow. Multiple flared, trumpet-shaped flowers to 2 in. (50 mm) wide in round clusters.
Plant hardiness: Zones 9–11. Ground hardy zones 9–11.
Soil: Well-drained. Fertility: Average. 6.5–7.0 pH.
Planting: Autumn or spring in partial shade to full shade. Space 6–12 in. (15–30 cm) apart, slightly below soil level. Space mature transplants 12–16 in. (30–40 cm) apart. In containers sized at least 2 in. (50 mm) wider than rhizome, one to a container.
Care: Easy. Keep moist. Tolerates drought. Fertilize in summer. Mulch. Propagate by offsets.
Storage: Indirect light, 40–60°F (4–16°C), in pot of dry–slightly damp soil.
Features: Good choice for beds, containers, mass plantings in indoor, woodland gardens.

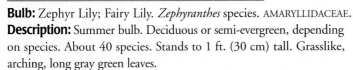

Bulb: Zephyr Lily; Fairy Lily. *Zephyranthes* species. AMARYLLIDACEAE.
Description: Summer bulb. Deciduous or semi-evergreen, depending on species. About 40 species. Stands to 1 ft. (30 cm) tall. Grasslike, arching, long gray green leaves.
Bloom: Summer–autumn. Pink, red, white, yellow. Solitary simple or lilylike flowers 2–4 in. (50–100 mm) wide with long, narrow, radiating, flared, oval petals. Some species are night blooming.
Plant hardiness: Zones 7–11. Ground hardy zones 7–11.
Soil: Well-drained. Fertility: Average. 6.0–7.0 pH.
Planting: Spring in full sun. Space 3–4 in. (75–100 mm) apart, 2–4 in. (50–100 mm) deep.
Care: Easy. Keep moist during growth; dry for one month following bloom. Resume watering for repeat bloom. Fertilize during growth. Mulch, zones 7–8. Propagate by offsets, seed.
Storage: Dark, 50–60°F (10–16°C), in net bag or open basket of dry peat moss.
Features: Good choice for accents, beds, borders, containers, edgings, mixed plantings in meadow, natural, rock gardens. Naturalizes, zones 9–11. Deer, rodent resistant.

Climate and microclimate govern bulb choices and when gardens are planned and planted

Plant Hardiness Around the World

The United States Department of Agriculture's Plant Hardiness Zone Map provides a general guide to growing conditions in North America. It divides the continent into 11 zones based on the average minimum annual temperatures within each zone. This system has been adapted to other areas of the world [see maps, pg. 132–133]. The zones roughly predict which plants will survive in a given area. Because weather varies from year to year, the actual minimum temperatures may be lower or higher than are indicated on the plant hardiness map.

When you're planning a bulb garden, use the information contained in the map to guide your plant selections. First find your locale on the map, then identify your zone by comparing its color to the legend. Many growers include zone information on their plant tags and bulb packages for your convenience.

Remember, bulbous plants grow best in zones where they've adapted fully to the climate. It's possible that plants from warmer hardiness zones than yours may live and bloom in your garden during a series of warm-winter years, only to fail when a cold year is experienced again.

In addition to plant hardiness zones, consider the first and last frost dates in your area [see Approximate Frost-free Dates, pg. 132]. Hardy bulbs that are adapted to survive cold-winter temperatures still require a period of adjustment after planting to ward off winter's chill. Plant them well ahead of autumn's first sustained cold temperatures. For tender, warm-season bulbs—those that need planting temperatures of 60°F (16°C) or higher—wait to plant until spring arrives and the soil warms. Remember, however, that the average first and last frost dates for your area are general guidelines and should be used subject to experience and advice.

Moreover, neither zone maps nor frost charts can account for the effects of thermal belts, nearby bodies of water, topography, and other factors that create microclimates within your zone. Only careful observation will give you an accurate picture of the effects due to climatic conditions in your own backyard.

USDA Plant Hardiness Around the World
North America

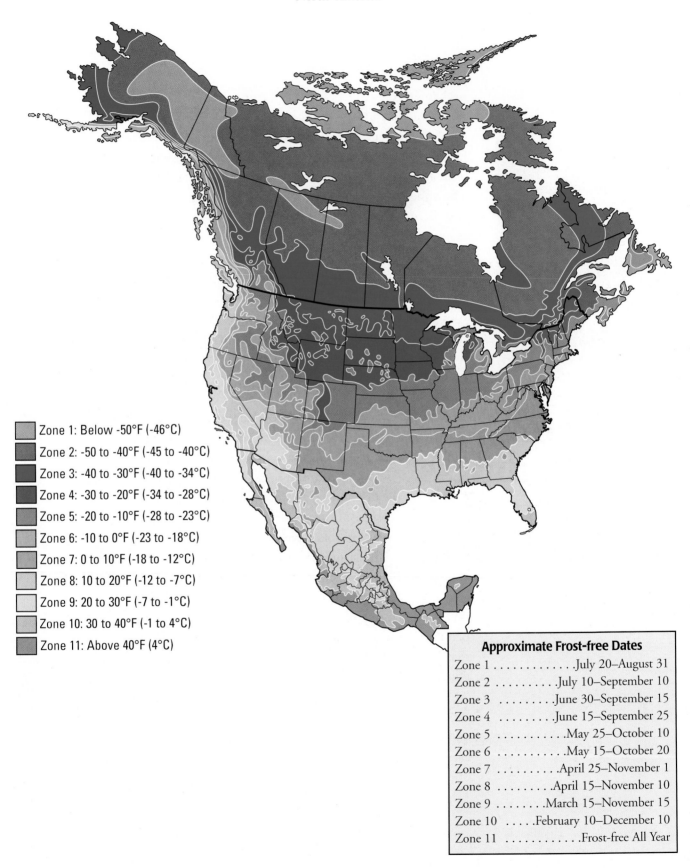

- Zone 1: Below -50°F (-46°C)
- Zone 2: -50 to -40°F (-45 to -40°C)
- Zone 3: -40 to -30°F (-40 to -34°C)
- Zone 4: -30 to -20°F (-34 to -28°C)
- Zone 5: -20 to -10°F (-28 to -23°C)
- Zone 6: -10 to 0°F (-23 to -18°C)
- Zone 7: 0 to 10°F (-18 to -12°C)
- Zone 8: 10 to 20°F (-12 to -7°C)
- Zone 9: 20 to 30°F (-7 to -1°C)
- Zone 10: 30 to 40°F (-1 to 4°C)
- Zone 11: Above 40°F (4°C)

Approximate Frost-free Dates

Zone 1	July 20–August 31
Zone 2	July 10–September 10
Zone 3	June 30–September 15
Zone 4	June 15–September 25
Zone 5	May 25–October 10
Zone 6	May 15–October 20
Zone 7	April 25–November 1
Zone 8	April 15–November 10
Zone 9	March 15–November 15
Zone 10	February 10–December 10
Zone 11	Frost-free All Year

USDA Plant Hardiness Around the World
Australia

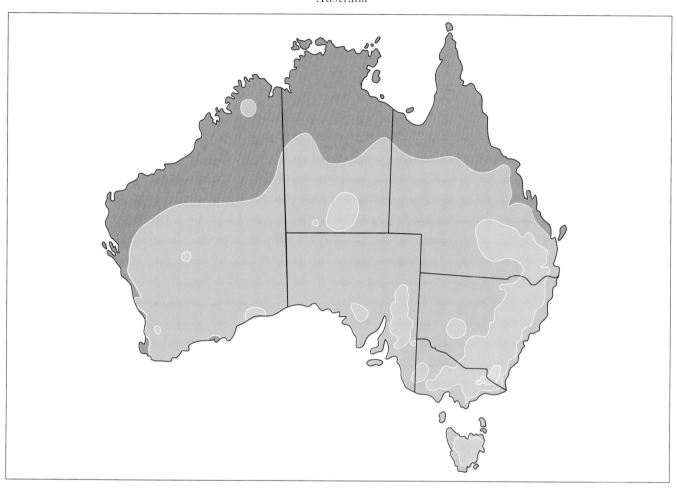

South Africa

New Zealand

Europe

ON-LINE   INDEX

I N D E X

I N D E X